running toward
DANGER

running toward
DANGER
Stories behind the breaking news of 9/11

By the

NEWSEUM

with Cathy Trost and Alicia C. Shepard

ROWMAN & LITTLEFIELD PUBLISHERS, INC.
Lanham • Boulder • New York • Oxford

ACKNOWLEDGMENTS

This book was created by the Newseum, the world's first interactive museum of news (www.newseum.org).

Chief copy editor was Ann Rauscher. Research and other copy editing: Christy Jerding, Don Ross, Sharon Shahid, Deborah Stoudt, Nancy Stewart, Jerrie Bethel, Mary Glendinning, Rick Mastroianni, Max Brown, Kristi Conkle and Kathryn Zaharek. Other help was given by Wendy Doremus, Rafe Sagalyn, Ken Crawford, Mike Machado, Sonya Watson, Shelby Coffey and Chip East.

Photo Credits:

Pages xiv-xv: James P. Blair/*Newseum*; Pages 18-19: Chao Soi Cheong/*The Associated Press*; Page 20: *CNN*; Pages 36-37: Naomi Stock/*Landov*; Page 38: *ABC News*; Pages 56-57: Patrick Witty; Page 58: *CNN*; Pages 68-69: Daryl Donley/*Photo Associates News Service*; Page 70: Courtesy *NBC News*; Pages 82-83: Gulnara Samoilova/*The Associated Press*; Page 84: Courtesy *NBC News*; Pages 110-111: Richard Drew/*The Associated Press*; Page 112: *CNN*; Pages 142-143: Mark Stahl; Page 144: *CNN*; Pages 166-167: Doug Kanter/*Agence France-Presse*; Page 168: *CBS News*; Pages 182-183: Luis Lujan; Page 184: *ABC News*; Pages 206-207: Ting-Li Wang/*The New York Times*; Page 208: *Telemundo*; Pages 220-221: Suzanne Plunkett/*The Associated Press*; Page 222: *Fox News Channel*; Pages 232-233: Krista Niles/*The New York Times*; Page 234: *CNN*.

Previous page: Agence France-Presse photographer Stan Honda at Ground Zero, Marilynn K. Yee/*The New York Times*; **Page VIII:** *New York Post* photographer Gary Miller stands on Liberty Street in New York City, Michael Norcia/*New York Post*.

Editors: Susan Bennett, Margaret Engel
Art Direction and Cover Design: Maya Vastardis
Design Assistance: Julia Wyatt
Photo Research: Karen Wyatt, Indira Williams, Megan Garnett

ROWMAN & LITTLEFIELD PUBLISHERS, INC.
Published in the United States of America
by Rowman & Littlefield Publishers, Inc.
A Member of the Rowman & Littlefield Publishing Group
4720 Boston Way, Lanham, MD 20706
www.rowmanlittlefield.com

P.O. Box 317
Oxford
OX2 9RU, UK

Distributed by NATIONAL BOOK NETWORK

British Library Cataloguing in Publication Information available

Library of Congress Cataloging-in-Publication Data

Trost, Cathy, 1952-
     Running toward danger: stories behind the breaking news of 9/11 / Newseum; with Cathy Trost and
     Alicia C. Shepard; foreword by Tom Brokaw.
          p. cm.
     ISBN 0-7425-2316-0
     1. September 11 Terrorist Attacks, 2001. 2. September 11 Terrorist Attacks, 2001—Personal narratives.
     3. Terrorism—Press coverage—United States. I. Shepard, Alicia C., 1953- II. Newseum. III. Title.

     HV6432 .T76 2002
     973.931-dc21   2002008480

Printed in the United States of America

Contents

Foreword | TOM BROKAW
ANCHOR AND MANAGING EDITOR, NBC NEWS

For most journalists, on most days there's never a shortage of good stories or important issues to cover, from the police beat to the corridors of power in the public and private sectors. They document and analyze the large and small developments that affect the lives of their readers and audiences, providing what has been famously called the first rough draft of history. That function is so critical to the health of a free society that the Founding Fathers had the wisdom and foresight to protect it in the First Amendment to the U.S. Constitution in plain, unequivocal language.

Yet, for all of their constitutional privileges and daily responsibilities, we know the press, print and electronic media are imperfect, occasionally slipping into self-indulgence or apathy or carelessness when the news becomes routine or there's an absence of the events that truly alter history's course.

The months leading up to September 11, 2001, were just such a period for the American press. There was simmering debate about news budget cutbacks, stories that were more titillating than enlightening and a diminished appetite for foreign news or developments in Washington.

Shortly before 9 a.m. Eastern Daylight Time on September 11, that debate ended when a hijacked airliner flew into the World Trade Center in Lower Manhattan, the first shocking development of a day unlike any other in our history. Instantly, the news media responded in a thoroughly professional, tireless and, in some cases, heroic fashion to provide information about what was happening, why it was happening and to thoughtfully discuss what may happen next. It was not just a big story. It was a transcendent event with immediate and enduring global implications, and political and economic consequences on a major scale. It is also a very human story about loss and heroism, grief and recovery.

The press coverage was and continues to be magnificent. It was as if every reporter, editor, producer, editorial assistant, intern, publisher and network executive was connected to the same brain wave. This is what we're to do and if we don't do this well, we have lost our place.

We haven't been perfect, of course. And the story is not over. But the compact between citizens and their press has been repaired and restored to its rightful place. I trust both parties will be vigilant about sustaining this relationship at a standard that will meet the test of history's judgment. ∎

Introduction

Driving to work, maybe you heard the news on the radio. Or at the office, your online news service sent an e-mail alert. Or someone called and yelled, "Turn on the television! You won't believe what's happening!" Wherever you were on September 11, 2001, you got news of the deadly terrorist attacks from the news media.

Live television provided unprecedented coverage of the attacks that killed nearly 3,000 people. TV networks stayed on the air with continuous news coverage for four days — the longest stretch for a single news story in television history. Nearly 80 million viewers watched prime-time broadcast or cable television news on September 11. Untold numbers listened to the radio, logged onto Internet news sites, or read one of the "extras" that more than 100 newspapers rushed to the streets that afternoon.

While every journalist, in a sense, has spent his or her career gearing up for the Big Story, no one was really prepared for this. How could anyone be? One unthinkable event followed another. Yet without hesitation, journalists in New York, Virginia and Pennsylvania — even those traveling with President Bush — ran toward danger. Many were frightened, but most didn't think twice. Julie Dreher knew better than to ask her husband, *New York Post* columnist Rod Dreher, not to race toward Lower Manhattan after the second plane hit the World Trade Center. "She knows that there are three kinds of people who run toward disaster, not away — cops, firemen and reporters," he said. That reply became our theme.

For this book, more than 100 journalists shared their minute-by-minute experiences covering the events of September 11. Their accounts contain intimate details, such as the marathon high-wire work of television anchors Tom Brokaw, Peter Jennings, Dan Rather and Aaron Brown, and the dramatic story of the evacuation and life-or-death experiences of journalists at *The Wall Street Journal*, the largest news organization closest to the World Trade Center. The book also features many rarely seen photographs of journalists in action that day.

"Running Toward Danger" includes stories of journalists who were physically injured or emotionally scarred as a result of covering the disaster, and a wife's story of how her photojournalist husband, William Biggart, died covering the collapse of the second tower. Six television broadcast engineers also died working at their posts atop the 110-story World Trade Center complex. They were: Gerard "Rod" Coppola, WNET-TV; Donald DiFranco,

WABC-TV; Steven Jacobson, WPIX-TV; Robert Pattison, WCBS-TV; Isaias Rivera, WCBS-TV; and William Steckman, WNBC-TV.

Within days of the attack, we began interviewing journalists who covered the disaster. Many were still shaken, though they downplayed their own bravery in deference to the hundreds of rescue workers who perished trying to save lives. Most journalists believed they had a responsibility to document the terrible tragedy in pictures and words. Their personal accounts are testimony to that determination and provide a glimpse of how newspeople fulfill their missions under enormous stress. These stories are edited excerpts of the interviews.

On this day of unimaginable fear and terror, journalists acted on instinct: they commandeered taxis, hitched rides with strangers, rode bikes, walked miles, even sprinted to crash sites in New York City, at the Pentagon and in Shanksville, Pa. "This was not some brilliant editorial mobilization," said Jonathan Landman, metropolitan editor of *The New York Times.* "People knew what happened, and they went. You can't plan for the World Trade Center falling down. You'd just better be ready."

Without the news media's determination, information about the attacks would have been scarce and sketchy. Instead, journalists reassuringly provided details to calm and to inform a terrified nation. Where would we have been without television? Television anchors provided constant news and context, carefully avoiding speculation or rumor that could heighten fears. Remarkably few mistakes were made on a day when chaos ruled.

According to a Pew Research Center poll, approximately 81 percent of Americans turned to television and radio September 11. TV networks aired no commercials for 93 hours, losing tens of millions of dollars in advertising revenues. Petty competition vanished. In an unprecedented move, cable and broadcast presidents quickly hammered out an agreement that morning to share footage for one day. Newspapers around the country also tore up budgets to throw resources at the story. Television got us through the first day, but newspapers and newsmagazines provided next-day context and analysis of what had gone wrong. Newsmagazines tore up planned issues to put out special editions.

On September 11, journalists faced four central challenges — logistical and communications problems, ethical dilemmas, risks to personal safety and emotional distress.

Reporting the story that day was a nightmare. Simple tasks such as calling authorities to get information or trying to get news stories to editors were stymied by a strained communications system. In the New York area, the attacks knocked out 10 cellular towers and disrupted 200,000 phone lines. Cell phones worked rarely or not at all. Photographers who used digital technology had to search for working phone lines to transmit images. When the planes struck the World Trade Center, many New York City television stations lost their transmitters and antennas, which were atop the complex. Television stations switched to backup systems or broadcast over cable lines or satellite.

Getting information from the Internet proved problematic for journalists. Yet, overall, the Internet performed admirably. For many journalists, it became a more reliable way to communicate than the telephone. Ironically, the Internet was created about 40 years ago as a way for the military to communicate in case of a nuclear attack.

Transportation was a quagmire. Traffic in Lower Manhattan came to a standstill. Bridges and tunnels in and out of the city were closed. Police closed roads and bridges in and around Washington too. After the Federal Aviation Administration halted all air traffic, news organizations rented cars to drive to New York, Virginia and Pennsylvania. Two *Los Angeles Times* photographers drove nonstop from California to New York, taking turns sleeping and driving.

No news organization was affected by the attacks as much as *The Wall Street Journal.* Because the newspaper's offices were so close to the World Trade Center, its reporters and editors were some of the earliest eyewitnesses to the carnage. The *Journal* ordered its offices evacuated at 9:03 a.m., just seconds after the second hijacked airplane struck. For a time, the newspaper's top editor was feared dead. Key staffers set up a makeshift newsroom by expanding a test newsroom at Dow Jones' corporate complex some 50 miles away in South Brunswick, N.J. The newspaper reached all but about 10 percent of its 1.8 million subscribers and produced an astonishing 32-page, two-section paper, winning the 2002

Left: Journalists walk along an ash-covered street after the World Trade Center collapse in New York. Center: A photographer prepares to take a shot of a victim after the Pentagon in Arlington, Va., is attacked by a hijacked plane. Right: ABC News Correspondent Ann Compton and other reporters watch coverage of the terrorist attacks while aboard Air Force One.
Page viii: *New York Post* photographer Gary Miller chronicles the aftermath of the terror attacks at the World Trade Center.

Photos left to right: Tricia Meadows/Globe Photos, Gerald Herbert/*The Washington Times*, Doug Mills/The Associated Press.

Pulitzer Prize for its coverage of the terrorist attacks of September 11.

Delivering newspapers in the disaster's aftermath posed another challenge. By midafternoon, New York City's four major newspapers faced seemingly insurmountable problems. *New York Times* publisher Arthur Sulzberger Jr. called New York Gov. George Pataki for help delivering papers from printing plants outside Manhattan, and the governor responded. At 3:30 a.m. on September 12, after dogs sniffed the contents, a caravan of newspaper delivery trucks rolled across the Queensboro Bridge into Manhattan under police escort.

Journalists also faced ethical dilemmas reporting the story. Usually reporters arrive after a tragedy. On September 11, reporters covered events as they happened, a situation requiring split-second ethical decisions and caution about reports that were hard to confirm. Police and fire officials established perimeters around the attack sites, forcing many reporters to fight for access. In Pennsylvania, only a handful of journalists reached the site of the plane crash.

Instances of cooperation between police and reporters occurred, but so did skirmishes, as journalists fought to gain entry to areas they believed they had a duty to cover. In New York and at the Pentagon, some journalists ripped off press passes and slipped through as civilians, or hid from authorities, but most openly declared their intent.

Journalists also struggled with internal and organizational ethics codes. They saw things no one should see and wondered if they should report them. Though many were sickened by the sight of people jumping or falling from the towers — and a few photographers refused to record the images — others argued that capturing the plight of those helpless people was a critical part of the story.

Journalists also grappled with the ethics of interviewing and photographing people in extreme distress. Many tried to balance compassion with the need to record one of the most powerful stories of our time. Many journalists risked their lives. They stayed close to the burning towers, taking gripping video and photographs that were relayed around the world. Most photojournalists acted on war photographer Robert Capa's famous dictum: If your pictures aren't good enough, you aren't close enough. When the first tower fell, photographers who had never run from a shot before ran like hell. When the danger passed, they went back.

Scores of journalists got caught in the hailstorm of debris and glass that rained down when the towers fell. Many envisioned they would suffocate to death in the choking dust cloud that swept over them. Flying beams and glass seriously injured several photographers. Others were bloodied and bruised. Most kept working.

Reporters on Air Force One were flown to secret locations with President Bush, never knowing where they were headed or whether the plane could be a terrorist target.

Emotionally, it was a day like no other. They were reporters, but what they were covering was happening to them, too. They struggled with fears for their lives and their families. Many said they straddled the line that day between being reporters and being victims. At the Pentagon and in New York especially, they were as much a part of the story as those they were covering.

For some, it was a day when their years of training and experience helped them operate almost mechanically. But for many others, the horror was often too much. Some agonized about people they knew who worked at the World Trade Center or the Pentagon or who were aboard the hijacked planes. They lied about where they were to reassure their families. Some journalists, overcome by the magnitude of what they were witnessing, cried on the air. No one criticized them.

At the end of the day, many tried to shake off memories of what they had seen — the heartbreaking dives of people without choices, a terrible 30-foot-deep gash in the ground left by a crashed plane in Pennsylvania, a stricken man searching for his wife at the Pentagon, and the charred photograph of a mother and her baby that floated down from one of the towers. But the next day most started working again, dedicated to delivering the news to a world that was hungry for explanations in the midst of madness.

The interviews in this book are arranged chronologically, as journalists describe where they were and what they were doing as events unfolded throughout the day. Although some of these newspeople have moved on to other jobs, the titles and news organizations listed with each name indicate that person's position and affiliation on September 11. Each chapter is introduced with a breaking news report, which appears as part of the timeline that runs throughout the book. Entries in the timeline indicate the specific time that events were reported by news agencies rather than the time they actually occurred. In the early part of the day, news broke at a hectic pace, reflected in the timeline's minute-by-minute descriptions. Later in the day, the timeline slowed as reports became less frequent.

The Associated Press, in particular, became the eyes and ears for thousands of news organizations on September 11. The AP uses four levels of notification to alert subscribers to a story's importance. The highest level is a flash, followed by an AP NewsAlert, a bulletin and an urgent. On September 11, the AP sent two flashes, 25 AP NewsAlerts and 18 bulletins.

On September 11, the news media provided the caliber of public service that journalism honors as its highest calling. They reminded us why our nation's founders gave journalists constitutional protections. At a time when public skepticism about the press was at an all-time high, the news media's steady performance renewed faith in the profession. In the words of former White House speechwriter Peggy Noonan, often a critic of the press: "They stood their ground and did their jobs," she said. "These men and women of the media should all get a mass Medal of Freedom the next time it's given. They really helped our country." ∎

Cathy Trost
Alicia C. Shepard

William Biggart | JULY 20, 1947 — SEPTEMBER 11, 2001

He picked up his first camera at age 14 and worked as an apprentice to commercial photographers to learn the trade. He dreamed of becoming a photojournalist but paid the bills with commercial jobs while he raised his young son by himself. Finally able to do the work he loved, he traveled to Gaza and the West Bank, Wounded Knee and the Berlin Wall. His name was William Biggart. He died covering the terrorist attacks on the World Trade Center — the only working journalist killed while reporting the story.

Fiercely independent in an industry increasingly dominated by big agencies, Biggart tried to preserve his professional freedom by aligning with a small progressive agency. Born in the divided city of Berlin where his father was in the U.S. Army occupying the city after World War II, he had a lifelong interest in political and international affairs. In his work, he was drawn to themes of division and conflict, including the divisiveness of Ireland, his ancestral country.

"What was a good day of shooting for Bill, most normal people would run from," says his wife, Wendy Doremus. "With a press pass around his neck and a camera bag slung over his shoulder, in the middle of the crossfire, this for Bill was heaven."

It was only natural that Biggart ran for his cameras shortly after learning from a shouted exclamation on the street that a plane had hit the World Trade Center. He and Wendy were walking their dogs near their home in downtown New York on a beautiful fall day, the first day of eighth grade for their son, Peter. Their daughter, Kate, was preparing to leave for a high school year abroad in Spain. Bill Biggart Jr., the son he had raised above his darkroom, was at work not far from the Trade Center towers.

Excerpts of Wendy's memories of that terrible day appear throughout this book. She spoke to her husband once by cell phone after the first tower collapsed. He reassured her, saying he was safe and with the firemen. She was never able to reach him again.

She spent the next days searching for him in trauma centers and hospitals. She faxed copies of his press pass to news organizations and hung "missing person" posters around the city. She stopped by fire stations, hoping that a rescue worker might have seen him. She did interviews with television stations "to get his name out there."

Late in the week, Wendy heard that bodies of several firemen had been found in the rubble, and a civilian had been found with them. She thought it might be Bill, though she couldn't verify it. She knew his passion for getting as close as he could to the people he photographed. His life's best work was portraits of the faces of hope and despair he found in Brazil, Northern Ireland, the Middle East and New York.

Wendy was losing hope but tried to keep a positive outlook for the children. "Bill was somebody who always came home," she says. "He was a Cancer, and like the crab, he loved his home. He would call constantly. We talked 10 to 12 times a day so I knew there was a problem if he hadn't called me."

On Saturday afternoon, she learned that her husband's body had been found in the rubble and was in the city morgue.

His three cameras, two camera bags, his notes, his press credentials, $26 and change, and his wedding ring were recovered with him. The cameras and press credentials had been singed and battered, but his final images were preserved on film and digital disk. There were 150 digital images and seven rolls of regular film, 290 images in all that traced his dogged path that day. His last image was taken just seconds before the collapse of the second tower — and his own death. Wendy wanted to go directly to the last shot to see where he was. "Do me a favor and cut to the chase. Show me the last shot," she said. "His last shot was taken at 10:28 a.m. He was right beneath the North Tower."

The North Tower collapsed at 10:28 a.m.

Bill was a storyteller who always came home to his family analyzing and discussing the news he was covering — tales that would be told "over and over again as great adventures," Wendy says. She is certain that if he had come home that night, he would have said "in typical black Irish humor: "Take my advice — don't stand under any tall buildings that have just been hit by airplanes." ∎

Preface | JOE URSCHEL, EXECUTIVE DIRECTOR, NEWSEUM

News matters. It matters because it fills a basic human need — the need to know. That universal curiosity has fueled the growth and speed of news gathering from ancient times to the present. When there is news of danger, news of death, of war, of destruction, that fundamental need ignites into a voracious and desperate craving for information that somehow will bring an understanding or explanation to the urgent question of the moment.

On September 11, 2001, the news was catastrophic. There was war, there was death, there was great devastation. And it was right on top of us. There was a desperate need to know throughout the country and the world. Who was bringing this terror to the United States? Why was this happening? And, of paramount importance, would we survive?

As soon as events began to unfold, and without a moment of deliberation, members of the news media rushed to answer those questions and thousands more in what has become the news gatherer's instinctive quest to know more and tell all. The contemporary news media have been studied and analyzed, fretted over and criticized. Their role has been questioned, their power challenged. News is now reported in an instant, if not live. News emanates from every corner of the world, and its collection process is often invasive and inescapable.

On September 11, all of that power and all of that speed were brought to bear instantly on the story that had nearly sent a nation into panic and hysteria. It was as if the news profession had been growing and evolving for centuries in order to be able to effectively report this story. There was no blueprint for doing it. There was no coordinated orchestration of resources. No one had anticipated a story like this, nor had they covered anything remotely like it. And yet, it would be nearly impossible to find another example of the news-gathering process working better or faster or more extensively.

This book is a description of how that almost imponderable process worked, hour by hour, minute by minute. This is the story of the storytellers. It is a story of chaos and calamity, but it also is a story of courage. The late Philip Graham, publisher of *The Washington Post*, aptly described journalism as "the first rough draft of history." To report on history you often must be an eyewitness to it. That is why reporters rush to the scene of the news when it is happening. Often, this puts them in dangerous situations. They go there to bring others the news, to answer those desperate questions and to satisfy the need to know. Sometimes, they don't return.

Photographer William Biggart was killed on September 11 in New York. The last frames on his film were of the North Tower of the World Trade Center collapsing. Before the end of the year, eight more journalists would be killed pursuing the story into Afghanistan. A few months later, Daniel Pearl of *The Wall Street Journal* would be kidnapped and executed in Pakistan.

These names join more than 1,400 others on the Newseum's Journalists Memorial in Arlington, Va., a steel and glass tribute to those who have died or been killed while trying to report the news. Some were covering wars. Some were reporting on criminal activity. Many around the world were killed by corrupt politicians and military thugs who disliked their reporting. Some were accident victims, simply in the wrong place at the wrong time. But most chose to go.

They went because they are part of a breed of storytellers who are inextricably drawn to the action — the news as it is happening, history as it is unfolding. That innate impulse even compelled fashion reporters — in New York to cover the fall shows — to flee the fashion district and speed downtown into the face of escaping crowds. They, and other reporters all over town, sent e-mails to home offices with messages such as, "I have my laptop and am headed toward the World Trade Center, what do you need?"

This is the story behind the stories of September 11. Revealing the story behind the news has been at the core of the Newseum's mission. As the world's first interactive museum of news, we have sought to foster a better understanding between the news media and the people they serve — to explore the role of a free press in a free society. The U.S. news media enjoy the greatest degree of freedom in the world — protected most broadly by the First Amendment to the U.S. Constitution. The biblical admonition that of those to whom much is given, much is expected, is particularly applicable to the press in America. We hold it to a very high standard, are quick to bemoan its lapses, critique it almost as public sport.

But in times of great calamity and tragedy, we turn to it immediately. We do so because we need to know, and we trust that we will be told. Much is expected.

On September 11, 2001, much was given. ■

8:52

8:53 A.M. **AP** NewsAlert: New York — Plane crashes into World Trade Center.

BREAKING NEWS

WORLD TRADE CENTER DISASTER

FUTURES: DOW ▲ 25.00   NAS ▲ 5.50   S&P ▼ 1.00   8:49a ET

CNN LIVE — BREAKING NEWS

WORLD TRADE CENTER DISASTER

Carol Lin: *"You are looking at obviously a very disturbing live shot there. We have unconfirmed reports this morning that a plane has crashed into one of the towers of the World Trade Center."*

MARK OBENHAUS | **Senior Producer**
ABC News

NEW YORK: As I approached the subway, I was facing the World Trade Center, and I heard this tremendous sound from behind me. I turned around and caught sight of this plane, which appeared to be flying extremely low. It was a massive, massive plane. The plane was suddenly looming over the building tops. It was so intense that we felt like ducking. You hunched down. It was clearly a commercial plane. I could not make out the details or any kind of lettering. Your eye just tracked it directly down West Broadway and right into the North Tower. It seemed in a second to just vanish in the building. The entire plane — wings, body, everything.

You could see this cavernous hole in the side of the building up 100 stories at least. Then the smoke starts billowing out. The whole experience felt like slow motion, but it probably took no more than five seconds. I immediately called my office on my cell phone. I said, "Cancel the meeting. Believe me, we are not going to be doing that meeting. Something terrible just happened down here."

> It seemed in a second to just vanish in the building.

LINGLING SUN | General Manager
China Daily Distribution Corp.

NEW YORK: I work on the 33rd floor of the World Trade Center North Tower. I heard this boom sound, and there was a violent shake of the building. My first reaction was that it was an earthquake. Then I felt a second boom. I hung up, ran out of my office, and it was deathly quiet. I saw dust coming out of the elevators and realized it's not an earthquake but an accident. There was a crash of the elevator. When I got back to my office, I saw a lot of people in the hall, shocked, motionless. I grabbed my ID and my keys and rushed to the fire stairs. I turned around to the people on my floor and said, "What are we waiting for? Let's go!"

We reached the 31st or 30th floor and there was this smoke. I didn't know if it was gasoline or rubber, but it was a terrible smell in the air. I couldn't open my eyes, and tears came down. There was a moment of panic. People didn't know what to do. People opened doors and tried to find a place where they could breathe. I went with them back to the office area. I pulled out my cell phone and called my husband. He was watching CNN. He said, "Honey, go! An airplane hit the building." He didn't know what kind of airplane; he didn't know it was an attack. He said, "Go down!" Just before I hung up, I heard him saying, "Oh, there's another airplane."

> ❝ What are we waiting for? Let's go! ❞

JOANNE LIPMAN | Weekend Journal Editor
The Wall Street Journal

NEW YORK: We were down there in the (World Trade Center) concourse when all of a sudden people started stampeding. People started saying that a plane hit the building. Typical New Yorkers that we are, we assumed that somebody clipped the antenna or some minor thing. But people were really running, so we got out the nearest exit, which was directly in front of the North Tower.

It was astonishing! As we walked out of the subway, it was snowing plaster and snowing financial papers, probably thousands of papers. It was like a really eerie kind of twisted ticker-tape parade pouring down from the sky. It was an incomprehensible scene. People were sitting there transfixed. We roused ourselves and said we have got to get back to the *Journal* office, which is across the street. We were thinking that this is the worst accident in the history of aerospace. We've got to get working.

When we got there, we actually couldn't get through because that's where the force of the blast had rained burning debris and twisted metal. Things were on fire in the street. We tried to wind across another little street, and it was even worse. There were pieces of the plane and also pieces of the passengers. We were picking our way through this debris when we realized suddenly it's not debris, it's what happened to the passengers. It was an unbelievable horror.

> We were picking our way through this debris when we realized it's not debris, it's what happened to the passengers.

Brian McKinley | Traffic Reporter
Metro Networks/Shadow Broadcasting

NEW YORK: I was getting ready for my last radio report about 8:45 a.m. We stopped feeding video to TV and started to turn for home. We were up by the George Washington Bridge. I go into my report about 30 seconds or so and as I'm starting to wrap up, I see the helicopter pilot waving frantically and pointing toward the front of the ship. I look up as I'm finishing the report and just saw the fireball. You just saw the black smoke.

It was when the first plane hit, right about 8:48 a.m. I'm finishing a report talking about delays at the George Washington Bridge and see this fireball. It seemed so unreal. It was mind-boggling. We just started flying toward it. Even as the words were coming out of my mouth saying, "There's an explosion near the top of one of the towers," I still didn't believe it.

WENDY DOREMUS | **Widow of Photojournalist** William Biggart

> He packed up his cameras and left.

NEW YORK: That was the first day our son was starting school. We had him go up to school, and we were walking the dogs. We noticed it was a very crystal-clear day, an almost alarmingly blue sky. It was about 8:45 a.m. I said, "Bill, look, there's an unusual cloud in this very clear blue sky." Then, typical New York, someone piped up on the street and said a plane just hit the World Trade Center. We went home. He packed up his cameras and left.

Pedestrians on the streets of New York react with horror to the terrorist attack on the World Trade Center on September 11.

Gulnara Samoilova/The Associated Press

DAN RATHER | Anchor and Managing Editor
CBS News

NEW YORK: I'd just stepped out of the shower. I'd been listening to a Willie Nelson album on a CD. I turned the radio back on to listen to the 9 o'clock news on WCBS. There were a series of bulletins. "Something's happened at the World Trade Center. It's believed that an airplane has hit it." My first thought is: Get moving.

BILL BEAM | Director of Engineering
WABC-TV

NEW YORK: There were nine over-the-air, full-power analog television stations and five digital TV stations broadcasting from the main antenna at World Trade at that time and four FM radio stations broadcasting as well. That was on the North Tower.

The top interior floor was 110. Above that there was a large flat roof, and built up off that roof was a 300-some-odd-foot tower with various antennas for the broadcasts. On the 110th floor were most of the broadcasters' transmitter rooms. One exception was WNBC on the 104th floor.

Don (DiFranco, WABC-TV's engineer) would have arrived on the 110th floor between 7 a.m. and 8 a.m. We have no indication other than that he was up there in our area by himself. (After the plane hit,) I know he spoke with someone in our master control, which normally monitors the signal in the transmitter. As far as I know, that was the last communication we had.

Our first reaction was we thought it was some kind of accident. We were trying to reach the Port Authority operations desk, where they dispatch fire and security teams, located in the basement of the World Trade Center. We called to make sure they understood we had personnel on the floor at that point. (Donald DiFranco was one of six television transmission engineers killed in the attacks.)

> Our first reaction was we thought it was some kind of accident.

WILLIAM F. BAKER | President and CEO
Thirteen/WNET New York

NEW YORK: There was a meeting of senior staff at 9 o'clock that morning and I was speaking by telephone from Canada. When I called in, my secretary said she heard that there was a terrible accident, a plane had hit the World Trade Center. When I got switched through to the conference room everyone was aware of it. I turned on the television in the conference room. When I saw the building that was hit, I saw smoke going up around the antenna and realized we were in jeopardy. More importantly, our engineer, Rod Coppola, was in jeopardy. He was on the 110th floor. When I saw smoke engulfing the area, I thought, "My God, he's above that area. That smoke must be really toxic. I hope he's getting out of there." We were asking if anybody had heard from Rod. We talked to the master control room and nobody had heard from him. Our lines of communication were down, but we were still on the air, so the presumption was that he was running this thing. Then our transmitter went out at about 8:50 a.m. About 70 percent of people in New York still had our signal (through cable), but millions of people couldn't get our signal. (Gerard "Rod" Coppola was killed in the attacks.)

> Our lines of communication were down, but we were still on the air.

ADAM LISBERG | Staff Writer
The Record, Hackensack, N.J.

NEW YORK: I live in New York City. For some reason I was up early, got into my car and turned on my ignition right at 8:48 a.m. when it happened. The first thought I'm ashamed to admit was, "Do I want to chase all the way to Lower Manhattan?" I knew I'd ruin my day and it would be a bullshit story.

I got our morning editor with my cell phone. She said, "Just take a ride by." I got around 40th Street and saw a plainclothes cop running in the middle of Ninth Avenue waving his badge in the air, trying to stop a couple of vans heading south.

I said, "Boy, this guy could do me a lot of good." He hops in. He was a parole or probation officer. I had just stopped at Starbucks and had coffee sloshing around in the cup holder. I probably picked him up at 8:55 a.m. or 9 a.m.

Mostly I was blowing red lights. I'm laying on the horn. I'm zooming between the curb and the buses. I blew every light I saw. I was going the wrong way down one-way streets. He's hanging out the window screaming at people, "Move, move, move!" and pounding on the side of the car.

> 'I'm zooming between the curb and the buses. I blew every light I saw. '

MARTIN WOLK | Business Reporter
MSNBC.com

NEW YORK: I sat down at a breakfast in the grand ballroom of the Marriott World Trade Center hotel. Suddenly the room starts shaking. The grand ballroom has tiny crystal light fixtures that covered the whole ceiling. They were shaking like an earthquake, only more. Everybody just ran out of the room full speed when we heard this muffled bang. I did what everybody else did. I ran to the lobby. I went to the front door and debris was raining down. People were saying, "Don't go out there."

RICHARD DREW | Photographer
The Associated Press

NEW YORK: I went to work to cover an early morning fashion show at Bryant Park. It was a maternity fashion show with pregnant models. I got there at 7:30 a.m. to do backstage fashion and I was shooting for an hour or more. I went out to the runway and the seats to stake out my real estate. CNN had a camera set up. The cameraman had earphones into the studio. All of a sudden he said, "There's been an explosion at the World Trade Center!"

My cell phone went off. (My editor) said, "Forget the fashion show! A plane just hit the World Trade Center and you've got to go."

' I remember looking outside and seeing people start to jump. I'll never lose that image. '

PAUL STEIGER | Managing Editor
The Wall Street Journal

NEW YORK: My first knowledge that anything was going on was when my wife called me. She works a couple buildings north for Lehman Brothers in the American Express Building. I was glued to my computer, and I didn't hear anything. She said, "What was that explosion?" And I said, "What explosion?" I was clueless. So I got up and raced to the other side of the building, looked out, and saw the flames pouring out of the first tower. And you know, right away I thought terrorism. I had not seen the plane. I just thought there was a bomb of some kind. I remember looking outside and seeing people start to jump. I'll never lose that image.

JIM PENSIERO | Assistant Managing Editor
The Wall Street Journal

NEW YORK: Paul (Steiger) said to me, "We might have to get out of here. What contingencies do we have?" And I said, "You can come to South Brunswick, (N.J.)." I had headed the project to put a new editing system in there. We had training rooms and had come down on Saturdays a couple of times and made pages. We had the capability to make the newspaper there.

GERALD M. BOYD | Managing Editor
The New York Times

NEW YORK: Publisher Arthur Sulzberger Jr. was throwing a party that night for Howell Raines, the new editor, and Gail Collins, the new editorial page editor. Invitations were sent out long ago. I decided to get a haircut. I stopped at a barbershop on the Upper West Side. I was sitting in the chair when people walked in saying that a plane had hit the World Trade Center. I leaped out of the chair and was dashing up the street with the barber chasing after me.

News photographers shoot pictures of Air Force One as it makes an unexpected departure from Sarasota-Bradenton International Airport with 12 members of the White House press corps aboard.

KHUE BUI | **Contributing Photographer**
Newsweek

SARASOTA, Fla., Traveling with President Bush: I went jogging with Bush at 6:15 a.m. Later I was driven to the school in the press van. We had these communication radios that can talk to other press vans. I heard there was a crash and that they needed to talk to (White House press secretary) Ari Fleischer. Then the radio went off again. It said, "President Bush needs to go to the holding room. He has a call holding from (national security adviser) Dr. (Condoleezza) Rice." It made you wonder what was going on. I was just thinking it must be something important if Dr. Rice was calling.

> ❝ I was just thinking it must be something important if Dr. Rice is calling now. ❞

BETH FERTIG | Reporter
WNYC Radio

> Oh, I'll just go cover this little fire and go to election night.

NEW YORK: I was supposed to be covering the primary (election) that night. I was still asleep when my acting news director called me just before 9 a.m. He said, "The World Trade Center has been hit. You've got to come in. We need you to find the mayor."

I had no idea what he was talking about. A few weeks before some crazy person tried to wind-sail into the Statue of Liberty, and I thought, "Oh, another nut case bumped into the World Trade Center."

I jumped into the shower. My boyfriend called. He said, "This is real! You've got to turn on the TV." It just wasn't registering. I turned on CNN and saw the visual of one tower burning, but it was still like, "Huh?" I still had the mind-set that I was going to cover the primary. I put on a suit and thought, "Oh, I'll just go cover this little fire and go to election night."

PARK FOREMAN | Technology Security
Consultant

BROOKLYN, N.Y.: The radio went to static. I happened to bend over by the window to turn off the radio. In a way, the absence of the radio was an indicator that something happened. I live in Brooklyn Heights. My living room faces northwest across the river and I can see the Trade Center and most of Lower Manhattan. I see the smoke and think it's a bad office fire.

I grabbed my Sony digital video camera and went up on the roof and stood there videoing for maybe five minutes after the thing hit. Smoke was traveling over Brooklyn with little pieces of paper landing on the ground and sidewalk like snow.

I zoomed in and realized there were bodies falling out of the building. You could actually see some of them tumble. I saw one guy clinging on tight to something and then fall. I saw four or five bodies. I have three on the video now.

TOM BROKAW | **Anchor and Managing Editor**
NBC News

NEW YORK: I'd been off most of the summer. A friend called the day before to ask how it was to be back. I said, "I'm doing fine, but there's no news. It's hard to get cranked back up." It looked like it was going to not be a terribly stimulating autumn. Social Security reform was the hot topic. The economy was winding down.

I was just finishing a workout at home when they called. I don't live that far, about 30 blocks uptown. The first thing I did was go look south. I live on the 14th floor. I thought, "Oh my God, this is a pretty big deal." I got dressed and ran outside. I remember thinking as I ran over to get a taxi, all these people don't have a clue what is going on downtown.

DAVID HANDSCHUH | **Photographer**
(New York) Daily News

NEW YORK: I was on the West Side Highway in Lower Manhattan probably one-and-a-half miles from the Trade Center when I saw the smoke. I always keep the police and fire radios on in the car. Just as I spotted the smoke, somebody comes on the fire department radio screaming about sending every available piece of apparatus in the city — a plane just crashed into the World Trade Center. My first thought was to call the office and let them know I was really close, that I can see the smoke. I was in a really good position.

On the way down I hooked up behind a fire rescue unit that was driving on the wrong side of the highway. I followed his rear bumper, driving right behind. I've covered the police and fire beat in New York City for over 20 years, so many of these men and women in public service are friends. Two of the guys are putting on their gear in the back of the truck, they're getting their tools ready and putting on their air tanks, and they're waving out the back window. It was their final run.

> ❝ I can see the smoke. I was in a really good position. ❞

9:04 A.M. AP — EXPLOSION ROCKS SECOND WORLD TRADE CENTER.

CATHERINE FITZPATRICK | Fashion Writer
Milwaukee Journal Sentinel

> We had a hole in the building made by a plane and that was all we knew.

NEW YORK: Our photographer, Rick Wood, and I came in on Saturday morning, very early as we almost always do during Fashion Week. They were showing spring 2002 clothes, and there were about 1,800 registered press from around the country and world.

I flipped on the "Today" show. I called my editor at home and asked, "Do you have the TV on?" She turned it on, looked at the TV and said, "Go! Go! Go!"

You get dolled up for Fashion Week, but I knew enough to wear comfortable shoes and socks. You have to understand we had a hole in the building made by a plane and that was all we knew. This happened blindingly fast.

Moments after stepping off the subway at 14th Street, workers in downtown Manhattan walk away from work, overcome with emotion. At right, *Milwaukee Journal Sentinel* reporter Catherine Fitzpatrick takes notes while recording the emotions of the moment.

Rick Wood/*Milwaukee Journal Sentinel*

9:05

SARA KUGLER | Writer
The Associated Press

NEW YORK: I usually leave the office around 8:30 a.m. When I got out of the subway, the first plane had already crashed. I started walking uptown and noticed a small group of people looking downtown and pointing. I could see the top of the tower on fire. I pulled out my cell phone and called the office. Kiley Armstrong said, "Sara, get to the World Trade Center. We think an airplane has hit it."

I got back on the subway. It was still running. Nobody was on the train. When I came out, people were standing there watching, not moving. I'd stop and interview eyewitnesses every time I heard something interesting. I was moving down Church Street when I saw FBI and NYPD running down the street with jackets that said "Joint Terrorist Task Force."

KILEY ARMSTRONG | Assignment Editor, New York Bureau
The Associated Press

NEW YORK: I was able to call (police reporter) Donna De La Cruz at home, and other people started to make calls. We couldn't get through to the Port Authority. Donna used her sources to confirm it. Sara Kugler was on her way downtown after working an overnight shift. This is the AP way — it's almost like you sleep with your fire boots next to your bed and jump up and start running. They just started calling the desk and saying, "Where do you want me to go?"

> This is the AP way — it's almost like you sleep with your fire boots next to your bed and jump up and start running.

ROD DREHER | Columnist
New York Post

NEW YORK: I had received a call early that morning from my city desk asking if I wanted to cover a potential strike by Catholic school teachers. "Maybe," I said, "I'll call you back," and I went back to sleep. Then my father called from Louisiana

> There are three kinds of people who run toward disaster, not away: cops, firemen and reporters.

to tell me. I went outside. The wind was coming out of the west, blowing the smoke toward us. There was a shimmering, glimmering air bridge of papers stretching all the way over from the towers to Brooklyn. It was really a beautiful thing. A horrible beauty, but striking. An airplane ticket landed in the back yard. It was from May.

We live on the Brooklyn waterfront, a straight shot across the harbor. I opened the front door, and there was the first tower on fire. I remember putting my hands on my briefcase when I heard the second explosion. I kissed my wife and boy and said, "I'm going to try to get as close as I can."

She didn't beg me not to go. She knows that there are three kinds of people who run toward disaster, not away: cops, firemen and reporters. I ran toward the Brooklyn Bridge; it takes 15 minutes. I stopped at an Arab-owned bodega where I always stop to get a bottle of water, because I figured I'd be down there for a while. People were running out of the store yelling, "My God, my God! The tower is on fire!"

AL ORTIZ | Executive Producer and Director
Special Events, CBS News

NEW YORK: I was in the newsroom talking to the national editor when I heard shouting from the news desk that a plane had hit the World Trade Center. "The Early Show" works out of a different building, so I immediately called Bryant Gumbel and told them to stay on the air. We went into special report mode and took over the network so that every CBS station across the country would get the same thing. That happened right after the first impact.

We threw together a staff of people close by who were already in the building. Between technical and editorial personnel, maybe a couple dozen people just could not get in to the city. We borrowed people from the weekend news, magazine shows and other CBS productions. We borrowed the booking staff from "The Early Show." We were flying by the seat of our pants.

MARTIN WOLK, NEW YORK: Alarms were going off. Hazy brown smoke was filling the Marriott lobby, which is in between the two towers. I felt it would be ridiculous to go back for my phone. I wasn't afraid. I never had time to think about my personal safety.

We exited south to Liberty Street. I started running around looking for a phone. In Two World Trade Center, across the street, I found a big bank of phones deep in the lobby. I called MSNBC's office in Fort Lee, New Jersey, so someone could take a little dictation. I gave him four sentences. He said to call back when I got a little calmed down.

I managed then to call my wife in Seattle. She told me to come home immediately. I said, "I can't." There were about 20 people on the phones. Suddenly everyone drops the phones and runs outside. I was so absorbed in the conversation with my wife that I was oblivious. Then I went outside and saw that the South Tower had been hit. Even after an eyewitness said he saw a full-sized plane slam into the second building, I did not believe it.

RICHARD PYLE | Reporter
The Associated Press

NEW YORK: Brenda (his wife) and I were watching the fire in the North Tower from our rooftop deck in South Brooklyn when the South Tower suddenly exploded in a huge orange fireball.

My first thought was that it had to be aviation fuel exploding, but I couldn't figure out why it was in the South Tower since the North Tower was the one that had been hit. Only minutes later did we realize it was an attack by yet another airplane. I called the office and reported what I was seeing.

Whether seen in person or on television, the image of those two jetliners slicing into the World Trade Center towers as if they were made of cheese does not compute. Even after covering six and a half wars, I have nothing to compare it with.

> ' I immediately called Bryant Gumbel and told them to stay on the air. '

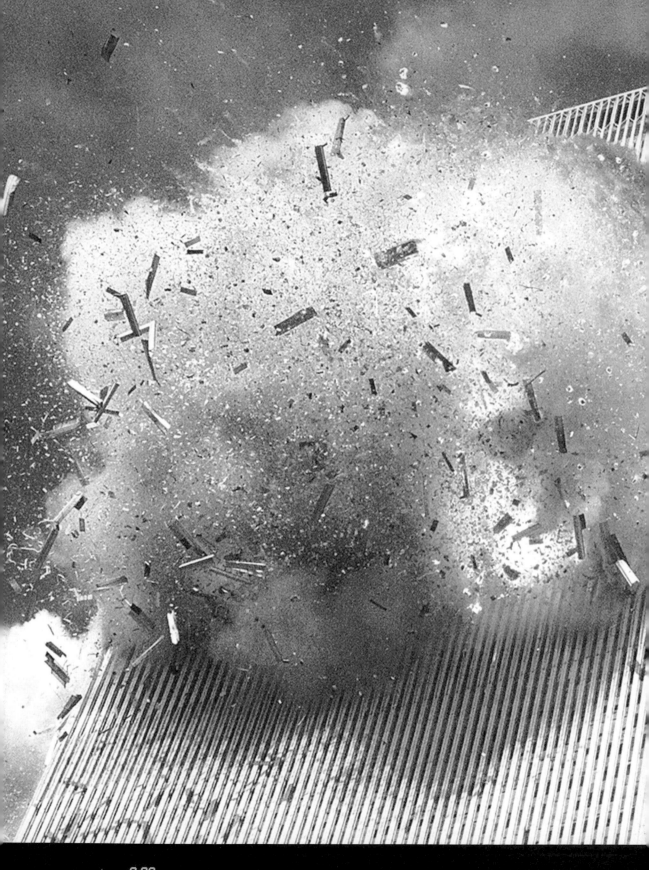

9:08

9:09 A.M. AP NewsAlert: New York — Plane crashes into second WTC tower.

ABC NEWS

"GOOD MORNING AMERICA"

Don Dahler (at the scene): *"Oh my God!"*
Charles Gibson (watching live shot on monitor):
*"That looks like a second plane has just hit! This
looks like it is some sort of a concerted effort to
attack the World Trade Center that is under way in
downtown New York."*

JOANNE LIPMAN | Weekend Journal Editor
The Wall Street Journal

NEW YORK: Just as we were crossing to our building (across from the World Trade Center), we heard this plane — the loudest plane you ever heard — and the explosion. Your animal instinct takes over. We dove for cover. The nearest thing was a parking garage with an overhang. We dove in there. At that moment, it instantly hits the crowd that this is no accident. This is terrorism. This area is under attack.

TOM BROKAW | Anchor and Managing Editor
NBC News

NEW YORK: I got in a cab, and while we were driving the second plane hit. We were listening to the radio. I thought they were making a mistake when they said a second plane hit, and that they meant the first plane. Then somebody came on the radio who I knew would have it right. Then I knew: This is terrorism, and this is a big, big deal.

I ran to the "Today" show set. They handed me wire copy as I went by. By the time I went on the air, there was not a lot more to know. We were reacting to what we were seeing.

> This is terrorism. This area is under attack.

JOHN BUSSEY | Foreign Editor
The Wall Street Journal

NEW YORK: I had gone up to the ninth floor and found an office right at the corner of our building where I could see what was going on. I got a line through to CNBC and started reporting to them. It was not at all apparent it was a terrorist attack, although this was presumed. We had a fire story. We had an incredible tragedy. I was reporting on the dimension of the fire and the rescue effort. Then the second plane hit.

I looked up as the plane entered the building because I heard an explosion. I saw debris and flame come blasting out of the South Tower. I thought at first that it was a charge, an explosive that had been put into the building.

ROBERT J. HUGHES | Reporter
The Wall Street Journal

NEW YORK: It was pandemonium on the street. There was stuff floating down and an awful smell of ozone and burnt stuff. We looked up stunned, then saw the second plane and the explosion. It was a cataclysmic explosion that TV couldn't duplicate. That's when people were truly frightened. We could feel the heat from the explosion. I thought immediately of the people up there. I thought I should be talking to the people who were escaping and getting their names, but I couldn't do it. I felt like such a failure. I couldn't put my wits together.

STEPHEN LUCAS | Director
"Today in New York," WNBC News

NEW YORK: April Amonica was giving her chopper report. That's when the second plane went into the second tower. Everybody in the control room at that point just froze and couldn't believe what happened. We knew at that point it wasn't just an amateur pilot hitting one of the buildings.

> Everybody in the control room at that point just froze and couldn't believe what happened.

JOHN DEL GIORNO | Helicopter Reporter
Metro Networks/Shadow Broadcasting, WABC-TV

NEW YORK: As we came out over Bayonne, New Jersey, we were climbing to 1,100 feet to get into controlled airspace, because it's just not as crazy up there. A plane flew by on the right side, less than a half mile away. All I could notice was that it was a passenger jetliner traveling north. This plane could have been on an approach into Newark, but it was just too low, traveling north, and traveling fast. Paul (Smith, the pilot) said to me, "Look at this yahoo flying into Newark like this." Paul was upset the air traffic controllers hadn't pointed him out.

The plane got just north of the Statue of Liberty and made a very abrupt motion. That's when the warning signs in your head start to go off. I've never seen a passenger jet make a dip like that. It dipped and then turned right. You knew at that altitude, at that speed, it wasn't a nice graceful turn, it was a turn. In the time it took us to process that information, that's how long it took for him to hit the second building.

As he went toward the building, I tried to get my camera over. By the time I looked down into the monitor, the monitor was just filled with fire. I said to Paul, "Did he just ...?" That's as much as I got out. Paul said, "Yeah, he just hit the building." That was as the city watched it live on TV from different shots. I immediately started screaming back to the newsroom, "A second plane just hit the building!" I'll never forget the disbelief in the assignment editor's voice. He said, "John, what did you say?" With that we lost all our radio communication with the station. We went off the air because all our transmitters were on top of the World Trade Center. The picture went to snow, and that was it.

The journalistic competitiveness that's always there — where you want to get the story first — was gone. You were just trying to figure out what was happening. In the back of your mind was the question of how to report this, knowing the whole city just watched this. How do you do this without creating absolute panic?

> The journalistic competitiveness that's always there — where you want to get the story first — was gone.

Robert A. Cumins/Black Star

Photographer Robert A. Cumins captured the second hijacked plane as it approached the South Tower of the World Trade Center.

ROBERT A. CUMINS | Documentary Photographer
Black Star

VERONA, N.J.: I live in a high-rise on a mountaintop above Upper Montclair, New Jersey. I was running late that morning. When I drove to the bottom of the hill, I realized that the radio wasn't on. I turned on the radio and heard this report on WCBS 880 where a helicopter pilot was talking about a tower that got clipped by a plane or something. The helicopter flipped it back to the studio, and the anchor said, "You've just heard that something major is happening at the World Trade Center."

The light was getting ready to turn green and I had a choice to make. There was something that told me to go back. (He becomes emotional.) Give me a second. There are days that I get right through talking about this and days that I don't. My mother passed away a month before and was a news junkie

> There was something that told me to go back.

like me. Sometimes I think she was the one who told me to go back. I turned back and went upstairs — the apartment I share with my girlfriend on the ninth floor faces New York. The first thing I saw was the whole skyline 18 miles away and smoke pouring out of the building. I ran down two flights to my (other) apartment, grabbed my camera bag and reached underneath a pile for this 500 mm lens that I knew would be the right one to use. It was a lens that I had bought eight years ago that day for the sole purpose of taking a picture of the handshake between (Israeli Prime Minister Yitzhak) Rabin and (Palestinian leader Yasser) Arafat on the White House lawn.

I ran back upstairs, stepping out on the ninth floor terrace. As I was putting my lens on and film in the camera, I saw this plane coming from south to north with the skyline in the background. That's often the same view you get when planes are taking off from Newark Airport, and I didn't really think about how low the plane was. I made a few pictures and the plane happened to be in them. I made one shot quickly, another shot quickly, then all of a sudden I saw a fireball.

Everything was in complete silence at this distance. I made a few more pictures, went inside and turned the television on. People were screaming that a second plane had hit the building. I never thought about the plane I had seen. It just wasn't in my mind.

> As I was putting my lens on and film in the camera, I see this plane coming from south to north with the skyline in the background.

MARTIN WOLK | Business Reporter
MSNBC.com

NEW YORK: I tried to interview, but it seemed useless. My note pad felt useless. I just stood there in total shocked silence watching the building burn. Then people started jumping off the North Tower. I used to work for Reuters for 10 years, so instinct kicked in and I started counting the number of people jumping. I had this sick feeling in my stomach. There's something wrong with watching people jump to their deaths, and counting them. I felt nauseated, very queasy. I could have stayed around, but I didn't see the point. I started walking.

RICHARD DREW | Photographer
The Associated Press

NEW YORK: I was avoiding the police, walking along West Street toward the northwest corner of the Trade Center. The police ordered me across the street to the World Financial Center, and I noticed a lot of ambulances and rescue people. I was taking pictures of the burning towers when a policeman standing next to me said, "Oh my gosh, look at that!" People were falling from the towers. We were watching a guy clinging to the side of the building on the North Tower while people were falling. I saw six or eight people falling from the building.

You know what you have to do. You make pictures.

There's one image I shot of a man falling headfirst from the building. I feel like the photo captured part of his life. We're here to tell the story. We don't edit for content.

> ❝ You know what you have to do. You make pictures. ❞

A man believed to be a Windows on the World restaurant waiter falls headfirst from the North Tower of the World Trade Center.

Richard Drew/The Associated Press

HAROLD DOW | Correspondent
"48 Hours," CBS News

NEW YORK: I was standing by ("48 Hours") executive producer Susan Zirinsky's office. She said, "Harold, come in here. Did you see what just happened at the World Trade Center? A plane ran off course and ran into the thing."

I said, "No, that was a terrorist attack." It was a clear day, and a plane would not just fly into it. That would be like hitting the lottery in reverse. Then the second plane came in and I know that it's a terrorist attack. Susan said, "Get your butt down there."

WILLIAM F. BAKER | President and CEO
Thirteen/WNET New York

NEW YORK: After the second plane hit, we knew it was a terrorist situation. I told our people to do what they would have done instinctively anyway — we are here as a public service to serve the people of our community. Do whatever it takes to do that. Forget the cost. Forget the inconvenience.

I said, "Remember first the kids of this community." Our worry was that during this great time of fright, what would the children do? Quickly, the station got into gear to think about programs to help them. The programmers took off our normal daytime schedule and loaded it up with kids' programs. We wanted to be a safe haven for kids.

> Do whatever it takes ... Forget the cost. Forget the inconvenience.

KHUE BUI | Contributing Photographer
Newsweek

SARASOTA, Fla.: (White House chief of staff) Andrew Card walked into the schoolroom where (President) Bush was listening to children read and told him. Bush looked white and was staring off, biting his lip and looking at his staff. You could almost tell that he wanted to end it right there. You just knew something serious was up.

AARON BROWN | Anchor
CNN

NEW YORK: I had gotten behind a police car and was simply following him. Then on the radio I heard the second tower has been hit, and I got it. I'm not the smartest guy on the block, but I got it. The police car, he just floored it. He was moving. I was right behind him. He was running lights and so was I. I got to 34th and parked the car. I was coming across Eighth Avenue and I'm running.

I remember saying to myself, "Just slow down." The one thing you don't want to be is out of breath. So I walked from the corner to here. I think the worst thing an anchor can do is to seem excited or breathless. I remember this feeling of extraordinary calm. From the time I got on this floor until I walked off at whatever time of night, 9 p.m. or whatever, I felt calm. Really calm. This is what you spend 30 years preparing to do. Without knowing the facts, I knew what to do.

> ❝ I felt calm. Really calm. This is what you spend 30 years preparing to do. ❞

JOAN ROSEN | New York State Photo Editor
The Associated Press

NEW YORK: I was driving into work listening to NPR (National Public Radio) when I started losing the station close to the George Washington Bridge. The announcer was saying that something had happened at the World Trade Center, and they had to get off the air because they were telling them to evacuate the building. I got through on my cell phone to Barbara (Woike) on the desk. "We're trying to get a chopper!" she said.

By now I can see the flames from the first one that hit, and I phoned downstairs to the national desk and said, "You've got to send people up to help Barbara because she's alone." I was going over the bridge and phoning Barbara again when the second plane, which I didn't see, hit the building. I saw the explosion. I screamed into the phone, "It's been hit again!" and Barbara yelled it out into the newsroom.

TODD MAISEL | Photographer
(New York) Daily News

NEW YORK: I was by Manhattan Community College when the second plane struck Tower Two. Police were screaming over the radio, "A second plane struck the Trade Center! We are under attack!" It didn't at first enter my mind that I was in danger, only that a great catastrophe was under way. Plane parts were on the ground. People were fleeing buildings in tears. Some were injured.

I raced to Liberty Street. There were body parts and luggage scattered on the ground. A human hand pointed at me on the pavement. Jagged parts of the plane were strewn about, one spearlike piece having pierced the hood of an auto. Cars were burning in the parking lot, and firefighters were attempting to put the fires out as small pieces of debris rained down from above. A firefighter was struck by something that fell from the building, his head and chest bloodied. Fellow firefighters were dragging him away from the danger, one screaming, "Hold on brother, hold on!"

> A human hand pointed at me on the pavement.

JIM PENSIERO | Assistant Managing Editor
The Wall Street Journal

NEW YORK: Around 9 a.m., I'm making phone calls and kaboom, the second one hits. That one I heard, that one I felt. I thought it was a bomb. I didn't know it was an airplane. This one didn't look as bad — famous last words.

(Managing Editor) Paul (Steiger) said, "We're definitely going to have to go. Finish up what you're doing." At that point there was the first announcement to evacuate our building. I went back to my office and typed up a fast e-mail to key people saying, "Both Trade Centers have been hit, and we think it's bombs. We're being asked to evacuate and move to South Brunswick (N.J.)."

At that point the second "evacuate the building" went out. I was just finishing this thing, when the security guy came in and said, "You've got to go."

SUSAN WATTS | Photographer
(New York) Daily News

NEW YORK: I'd just gotten there and, of course, was photographing everything in front of my eyes. I remember the exact moment I took this picture. The man was calling for help, and he kept looking up at the building. The woman who was injured was just clawing at him. It was this incredible interaction of strangers. Clearly these two people didn't know each other. He was obviously comforting her.

There's another picture of a man jumping out of the building, almost as if he's spread-eagled. His arms are out and he's face down. He has no shoes on. It's a terrifying picture for me to look at now. He looks like a bird, and it looks like he didn't

> The woman who was injured was just clawing at him.

An injured woman is comforted after escaping the World Trade Center.

Susan Watts/New York *Daily News*

fall out of that window. It looks like there was a decision made. It was frightening that people had to choose their deaths.

HOWELL RAINES | Executive Editor
The New York Times

NEW YORK: September 11, 2001, was my sixth day as executive editor. I was having a cup of coffee in my Greenwich Village townhouse on the bottom floor. I just happened to turn on CNN minutes after the first plane hit. Then I saw the second plane hit. Within two minutes my phone was ringing. It was (publisher) Arthur (Sulzberger Jr.), who said, "Are you watching this?"

That night there was a dinner (for top editors) that already had been planned. "Should we cancel it?" We decided, "Let's not." I went upstairs to take a shower, reached my second floor and thought, "Of course, we have got to cancel it." I showered as quickly as I could, left my house on 11th and walked to Seventh Avenue. I saw emergency staff outside St. Vincent's Hospital with gurneys and scrubs. They were waiting to receive the wounded. I saw pedestrians who were stopped and looking south. I crossed Seventh Avenue and saw smoke. My first thought was to run back to my house and get a camera. No, I'm the editor of *The New York Times*. We'll have photographers there.

Once I decided not to go back to the house, I stood and watched. I knew that this was the last time I was going to experience directly what was going on, then I would go into the news cocoon. Once you are managing the process, you really are not experiencing it directly.

If this had to happen, I'm glad I got to see the real-life scene. That helped me adjust to the magnitude of the event. I walked across to a deli. There was a taxi there. "Can you take me to Eighth Avenue and 43rd?" I asked. The driver said, "I need to find out where my daughter is." "I'll give you $20," I said. "Get in," he replied.

> ' I knew that this was the last time I was going to experience directly what was going on, then I was going into the news cocoon. '

RICARDO ALVAREZ | News Director
Telemundo/Channel 47

TETERBORO, N.J.: We had problems getting reporters there. We had two crews in New York covering the primary. We're in New Jersey, and a couple of other reporters had to go up almost by Yonkers, cross over the Tappan Zee Bridge and come down. We did have a contingency plan, but it didn't include having the bridges or tunnels closed.

GULNARA SAMOILOVA | Photo Retouch Artist
The Associated Press

NEW YORK: I'm thinking there must not be a lot of AP photographers there yet. I must go there and cover it. I work at AP and know the system — it's a news agency and you have to be fast. I'm shooting pictures while I'm walking. I'm in shock because I know now it is a terrorist attack. I'm across the street from the towers making photos when a policeman tells me to get out of there. He says, "Can't you see people are suffering? How can you take pictures?" I say, "I have to document it."

PETER JENNINGS | Anchor and Senior Editor
ABC News

NEW YORK: I have a colleague I work with in all of this. Nancy Gabriner. She knows instinctively what I want early on. What I want is precedence because the circumstances haven't revealed themselves yet. We have a plane flying into a building. She'll start diving for material. Has this happened before, etc.? The whole ABC operation gets involved, but Nancy is my right and left hand. We are joined at everything but the hip.

The very next thing I did was take an emotional and intellectual breath and say to myself, be careful. As we've said occasionally on the air, very often the first apparent facts are the wrong ones. I think that way all the time. I am a deeply profound skeptic.

> He says, 'Can't you see people are suffering? How can you take pictures?' I say, 'I have to document it.'

9:21 A.M. **CNN —** ALL BRIDGES AND TUNNELS IN THE NEW YORK AREA CLOSE.

GERALDINE BAUM | Reporter
Los Angeles Times

NEW YORK: My husband (*New York Times* editor Michael Oreskes) dropped me right in front of Times Square. He was going to *The New York Times* (offices). There's that huge television screen, and we saw the second plane hit. I started running toward the subway. He yelled my name. I looked back at him. He'd put out his hands, pointing. All of Times Square was at a standstill.

I jumped on the subway, pulled out my wallet and my police ID. My experience is you need to be wearing your credentials. I didn't have a chain. I started asking all the women, "Do you have a chain, a ribbon, a string, anything?" I'm 46 years old. I knew I was going to cover an event, and I knew what I needed. The train stopped at 23rd Street and it wasn't moving. I started running downtown. I was wearing slide shoes with no back. They were not something on which you want to be running for your life.

I decided to commandeer a car. There was a sense of panic in the streets. I felt it. I pulled a guy over. "Here's $40, please take me as far south as you can go. I'm a reporter." He only made it down to 14th Street. Then I was running down Seventh Avenue again. I saw a cab with a woman (passenger) in it smoking a cigarette. I got in her cab. She's yakking on the cell phone with her friend. I asked her, "Do you have a chain?" She found a safety pin and she safety-pinned my press badge.

I said to the driver, "Take me as far south as you can." She (the passenger) didn't mind. She was on her little adventure. I got out. I started walking. I saw the engine of one of the planes in the middle of Warren Street.

I kept going and going. You'd see somebody completely covered in gray, dust, dirt and grime and I'd stop to interview them. One guy, a businessman, I'll probably never forget. His button-down shirt was open. His hair was completely matted. He was staring straight ahead, his hand firmly gripped around this bulging briefcase. He was in some kind of daze.

> " Here's $40, please take me as far south as you can go. I'm a reporter. "

RUTH FREMSON | Staff Photographer
The New York Times

NEW YORK: It was rush hour. As I got into the car, I thought, "What can I do, realistically?" I was by La Guardia Airport. I called the desk and said, "Why don't you arrange for a helicopter, and I'll do the aerial shots." I got to the airport in five minutes. Just as I was pulling up to the terminal, I heard that the airspace was sealed off. I could see the smoke. I pulled over on the shoulder to call the desk and take a picture of the skyline. As I was pulling back onto the highway, a convoy of 10 to 15 emergency vehicles with sirens screaming, lights flashing, appeared. I got behind them and decided to stay with this convoy.

The cop in front was waving me to get back. Every time I saw the smoke, I knew I wasn't leaving them. At the same time, I'm listening to the radio. A man was describing what he had seen, and then he said, "Oh my God, here comes a second plane!" The police were starting to seal off the bridge and tunnels. Our company cars are these Chevy Luminas, which look like undercover cop cars. I was at the end of the convoy of clearly marked emergency vehicles, and they just waved me right through. That's how I ended up being taken immediately to the bottom of the World Trade Center.

> I pulled over on the shoulder to call the desk and take a picture of the skyline.

DAN RATHER | Anchor and Managing Editor
CBS News

NEW YORK: I had this argument with myself. Go down there. Try to be a field reporter for the time being, and maybe later in the day come back to anchor.

A lot of what I was thinking happened in nanoseconds. But my instructions were to come in here. In this kind of story, I can be of limited use. Whatever value I may have to CBS News and the audience, the people who depend on us, would be to try to bring my experience as a journalist and a broadcaster to bear. I arrived at CBS at 9:13 a.m.

JOHN DEL GIORNO, NEW YORK: We had no immediate radio contact with the station, but still had air traffic control radios. Our pilot said to Newark, "A second plane just hit the building," and Newark just very calmly said, "We saw it." We continued north on the Hudson River. At that point, you start trying to find the balance between being a reporter and being a person. You know this is a planned attack; your next thought, as you're 1,200 feet over the Hudson River, is, "Where's the next one?" In an aircraft, you start saying your prayers. You say, "I hope it's not behind me because if it is, I'm not going to see it." Our major concern at the moment was that there could be a third aircraft somewhere behind us at our six o'clock (position) where we couldn't see it.

I had no radio contact with the station, but I started feeding the video anyway. I figured they would figure it out. I did not know if we were totally knocked off the air, which it turns out we weren't — we were still feeding to the outside regions. We were off the air as far as the air signal goes, but we were still feeding cable, still feeding satellite for the most part. The idea was to stay out there and feed them, even if they're knocked completely off the air, because maybe the network will take it.

> You start trying to find the balance between being a reporter and being a person.

MARIANNE McCUNE | Reporter *WNYC Radio*

NEW YORK: I ran to the Manhattan Bridge and begged a bike messenger to give me a ride across. I rode on the seat and wore his backpack for him. He stood most of the time. Both towers were on fire, and there were tons of people walking across the bridge. There were a lot of schoolchildren walking. There was not a lot of traffic in the bike lane. He kept yelling, "Bike lane! Bike lane!" He left me at the Bowery because traffic was so bad. I ran down the street to the Municipal Building (which houses the WNYC offices), where I saw all my managers and the people who work at WNYC running out of the building.

MARTY GLEMBOTZKY | Photographer
WABC-TV

NEW YORK: I got there thinking: towering inferno, world's worst fire. I parked my truck, grabbed my camera, grabbed the microphone, and I grabbed my wallet because I really thought that I was going to be having lunch and had better bring some money.

I got into a small fight with a police officer. I had press credentials because I was used to the (Mayor Rudolph) Giuliani administration trying to prohibit us from access. We set ourselves across the street from the North Tower on the West Side Highway and just started doing our thing.

I felt something happen. I know it was somebody landing on the ground. I have to be honest that I pretty much shut down at that point, realizing that people were jumping. I saw people hanging out of the windows. I was trying to shoot what was going on, but I was horrified by what I was seeing. I was at a loss, professionally — I'm mildly embarrassed to admit.

FRANK SCANDALE | Editor
The Record, Hackensack, N.J.

> The first thing is making sure you get people there — as many as possible.

HACKENSACK, N.J.: I walked into the newsroom at 9:15 a.m. Tim Nostrand, assistant managing editor for assignments, was one of the main guys calling in the troops and sending them out. Everybody was walking around in disbelief. There was a lot of, "Oh my God." The first thing is making sure you get people there — as many as possible. You can always pull them back. We met after we had people deployed. Most of the people who live in New York City were hip to what was going on and were running to the scene. Vivian Waixel, the former editor and now VP in charge of the editorial division, has been in this newsroom 29 years. She came running into the newsroom saying, "Make sure the ads are cleared and let me know how much space you need."

BOLÍVAR ARELLANO | Photographer
New York Post

NEW YORK: I went to a place where nobody else was, across the street from the Number Two tower. The cops were pushing us away, so I went behind a fence and was hiding there taking pictures of the building. I was taking pictures of people jumping. The whole thing was very traumatic for me because, oh my God, there's nothing I can do. The only thing I can do is to keep taking pictures because that's my job.

I am a Catholic, and in the church they teach you that you don't have to pray out loud, that God can hear the thoughts in your mind. I was praying inside my mind, "God, give them wings so they cannot touch the ground. I know you are going to take them, but take their full bodies, not in pieces." It was the most traumatic moment of my life.

> It was the most traumatic moment of my life.

Bolívar Arellano/New York Post

A person falls from the 110-story North Tower of the World Trade Center.

9:26

9:30

9:31 A.M. AP NewsAlert: Sarasota, Fl. — Bush calls WTC crashes apparent terrorist attack.

BREAKING NEWS
BUSH COMMENTS ON WORLD TRADE
CENTER DISASTER

CNN LIVE

CNN

WORLD TRADE CENTER DISASTER

Leon Harris: *"President Bush is speaking (joined in progress)."*
George W. Bush: *"Today we've had a national tragedy. Two airplanes have crashed into the World Trade Center in an apparent terrorist attack on our country."*

ARSHAD MOHAMMED | White House Correspondent
Reuters

SARASOTA, Fla.: At the end of the photo-op with the kids, we were about 10 or 12 feet away from the president, right behind the second-graders. I called out to the president something like, "What can you tell us about the plane crash in New York?" He replied, "I'll talk about it later."

At one point, there was a rumor that he might go to New York, which made no sense because for the president to go anywhere diverts a tremendous amount of resources that would suck resources away from the tragedy. We got crowded into an auditorium and he spoke to the nation on television.

> ‘ I called out to the president, `What can you tell us about the plane crash in New York?’ ,

KHUE BUI | Contributing Photographer
Newsweek

SARASOTA, Fla.: After Bush's announcement, we scurried to the motorcade on foot and hopped into the motorcade. At this point, if you are not in the press van, they'll leave. On a day like this, the motorcade left pretty quickly. We knew we were going to the airport, but that was it.

9:32 A.M. **CNN — SOURCES SAY ONE OF PLANES IDENTIFIED AS AMERICAN AIRLINES 767.**

We got to the airport and Bush hopped out of the vehicle quickly. We were all running with all this equipment. I couldn't even get a cell phone connection to New York. I was carrying about 30 pounds. I had my clothes, camera equipment and extra film. But it was the wrong kind of film. I realized I was kind of screwed. I brought indoor film because that's what the schedule indicated, but we ended up outdoors.

DAVID SANGER | White House Correspondent
The New York Times

SARASOTA, Fla.: It was nearly half an hour before the president walked into the larger room where his speech was scheduled to take place, colorful posters behind him. I'll never forget the look on his face. By now, he was ashen. He almost twitched. He must have known his presidency had changed forever, that it would be measured from that moment forward by what he said, how he said it and how well he could calm the nation.

> He must have known his presidency had changed forever.

PAUL STEIGER | Managing Editor
The Wall Street Journal

NEW YORK: I called our Washington bureau chief and told him that we were going to have to be producing from South Brunswick (N.J.). Though we would have access to a lot of reporting from our area, his bureau would have to carry the lead in terms of conceptualizing stories and writing them.

I went downstairs, west of the World Financial Center, where there's a yacht basin and a pavilion as you go to the Hudson River. There were thousands of people milling around, watching what was going on as the increasing horror unfolded. I started looking for editors. I knew we needed to get editors across the river to put together a paper. Luckily, I ran into Larry Ingrassia and Larry Rout, two of the paper's best editors. I said, "Get across the river. Take the ferry."

SONYA ROSS | White House Reporter
The Associated Press

SARASOTA, Fla.: (President) Bush used the words "terrorist attack." I was trying to keep up with what he was saying to get the quotes right. I began to think that this day had taken a serious turn. I called our national desk in D.C. and got an editorial assistant and began dictating to her. Accuracy was all I was thinking about.

As soon as Bush finished, he said we were leaving Sarasota. We dashed to the motorcade and went straight to the airport. My sister Terea in Atlanta called my cell phone wanting to know where I was. I'm the baby sister of four daughters. Given that two planes had flown into two buildings and the airports were all closed, I didn't know what was in store in terms of how safe it was to fly. I said, "Of course, I'm safe. I'm with the president."

When we got to the tarmac, I called the desk with my cell phone and said we would probably get an update on the plane. I'm dialing with my thumb, holding my laptop and purse while I'm jumping out of the press van. I asked to speak to bureau chief Sandy Johnson. Sandy said, "A plane has crashed into the Pentagon. I gotta go."

Then I was scared.

> Of course, I'm safe. I'm with the president.

PARK FOREMAN | Technology Security
Consultant

NEW YORK: I took my video camera downstairs after both buildings were up in flames and loaded the video onto my computer. I couldn't use my telephone. I sent an e-mail to my brother Howell in Atlanta to tell him what I had. He had telephone service. He could conduct negotiations and find a buyer. When you see something like that, you know you can sell it. Maybe to CNN, I thought, they're in Atlanta. Howell started making calls.

TOM FLYNN | Producer
CBS News

NEW YORK: Between West and Battery streets, I found a Merrill Lynch guy who just got out of his building. He was (video) taping. I said, "You are now working for CBS." He said, "OK." I pulled one of my cards out and put it in his top left-hand pocket. We were together for 30 minutes. I was there five minutes after the plane hit the South Tower. Primarily, he was focusing on the towers. The fire in the North Tower became more and more of a conflagration. People were jumping all the time. I must have seen 50 people jumping. In one two-minute span, there were five people who jumped.

If you looked straight up from where we were, you could see the bent steel as it pushed in. You could see part of the plane, not the signature part of the tail with the fin, but a part of the plane that was blackened.

I didn't see people hit the ground. Some were coming through the smoke. They were 1,000 feet above the fire. It was windy. Some of them got blown back into the building. But it is an unreal vision. You are standing there watching people jump without parachutes, 1,000 feet up, and knowing they are going to die.

' You are standing there watching people jump without parachutes ... knowing they are going to die. '

JOANNE LIPMAN | Weekend Journal Editor
The Wall Street Journal

NEW YORK: I'm still thinking, "OK, I've got to get to the paper. We have to cover this story." We ran into one of our colleagues in the garage who told us that our building was already locked down and we wouldn't be able to get into it. So we made our way to the water, and several of us from the paper made our way carefully past the towers, again headed uptown. Everyone was on their cell phones trying to reach everyone else, and no one could get through to anyone.

MARTY LEDERHANDLER | **Senior Photographer**
The Associated Press

NEW YORK: I didn't go down to the site because my legs don't hold up so well. I'm 83; I've worked here for 65 years. I took my long lenses and went to the GE (General Electric) Building, up to the Rainbow Room. I got up to the window and made a bunch of pictures of the Empire State Building with the World Trade Center on fire in the background. Then they evacuated the building. I wish I could have hid someplace. I've covered everything from the riots in Newark to D-Day, the Kennedy inauguration to the Stork Club. I flew over Woodstock and helped get pictures out after the Hindenburg explosion. I covered the '93 World Trade Center explosion.

This one was about as bad as D-Day.

> ' This one was about as bad as D-Day. '

Photographer Marty Lederhandler's shot of the twin towers burning behind the Empire State Building in New York on September 11.

Marty Lederhandler/The Associated Press

9:36

JOAN ROSEN | New York State Photo Editor
The Associated Press

NEW YORK: When I got to the other side of the bridge, West Side Highway was blocked off. All the cars were stopped. I got out of my car and put on my press pass and asked people to help me move the car. I maneuvered it into a little area, and I just ran. The cops started screaming at me, "You can't go down that ramp!" And I screamed back, "I'm press!"

I climbed over a huge barrier and ran to Riverside Drive where I saw a TV truck from Channel 7 Eyewitness News. They saw my press pass and stopped and told me to jump in the van. They dropped me off at 52nd Street, and we wished each other luck. I saw a cab, but the driver was freaked out. He said he was going off duty. I asked him to please just take me to midtown. He took me two or three blocks before he said, "Please leave my cab!" I ran the rest of the way to work and got there at about 9:40 a.m.

BETH FERTIG | Reporter
WNYC Radio

NEW YORK: Our office is six blocks north of the World Trade Center, near City Hall. I raced upstairs and one of the station vice presidents was saying, "Get out of the building because it's been evacuated." Our morning host, Mark Hilan, was still on the air, and he was staying. I remember seeing my program director and saying, "I'm going to go down there." He said, "Don't do anything crazy." I started running down the street asking the police where the mayor was. They thought he had gone to his bunker at the old command center at Seven World Trade. I was thinking, "Oh my God, he's down there!" I started running and fighting through the crowd of people, thousands of people, around City Hall.

Both planes had hit, both towers were burning. I knew this had to be terrorism.

JOHN BUSSEY | **Foreign Editor**
The Wall Street Journal

NEW YORK: Security folks came up, along with one of the company officers, and said, "We need to evacuate the rest of the building." I felt that it was safe enough to stay. I said to the company officer, "Look, we're across the street from this." I was inside a building, looking out through glass windows, across the street from this thing.

If you think about it, foreign correspondents take much greater risks than what I was doing. Think about some of our colleagues who have gone into Vietnam and Kosovo and the Gulf War and Chechnya. These are infinitely more horrific and dangerous environments where people are intentionally trying to pick you off. At that time, I thought it was the right news judgment and the right decision.

TERRY SCHWADRON | **Editor, Newsroom Technology**
The New York Times

NEW YORK: We had a lot of things to do immediately. My part was logistics. I had to make sure we set up a war room. We took over a conference room, which actually was used by a group of volunteers from advertising who came down to take phone dictation. They started taking all the calls from outside as well as from reporters.

I set up some special baskets for copy within the first hour, a half dozen or so for everything that came in that day. We started working on making it possible for people to work from an emergency newsroom that we have in the printing plant at Edison, New Jersey. It's a big, dusty, un-air-conditioned, funky room with 50 desks. Normally, it's not used. It waits. It has computers, phones and connectivity to the Internet, to the (editing) system. We've had it for about four or five years. We do some fire drills there. But to my knowledge, it hasn't been used before.

> I had to make sure we set up a war room.

BRIAN McKINLEY | **Traffic Reporter**
Metro Networks/
Shadow Broadcasting

NEW YORK: We were on our way to try to get more fuel at another airport in northern Jersey. We were watching from a distance, then we heard on the pilot radios that F-16s were on the way. It takes on a higher level of importance. Normally, we're not involved with anything like that. We're just doing our little traffic gig.

We were almost on the ground at that point. It was reassuring in one sense that we were on the ground. But my friends and colleagues were up there at the same time, and you don't know if another plane was coming. You wondered, "Is somebody going to get shot down?" That's frightening, the unknowing. You know there's someone out there to protect you, but protect you from what?

SARA KUGLER | **Writer**
The Associated Press

> I realized that people had been blown out of their shoes.

NEW YORK: I actually found a working phone. I didn't know our 800 number, so I was feeding quarters into it. I gave dictation to Beth Harpaz. Mostly I gave color. As I got closer to Vesey Street, I saw men's shoes. Then I realized that people had been blown out of their shoes. There were computer bags, purses, desk items, pieces of computers. I realized they were from the building. It was my first moment of understanding that this wasn't just a building on fire. This is people. When I was talking to Beth, I noticed two places where bodies had been removed, but there was a pool of blood and brain matter still in an area marked off with yellow tape.

I was pretty calm. I had an inkling of what it was like in the office. They didn't need hysteria. That conversation lasted about five minutes. Beth wasn't telling me anything about what was going on and I didn't want to bother them.

BOLÍVAR ARELLANO | Photographer
New York Post

NEW YORK: I saw (photographer) Bill Biggart. I was across the street (from the towers). I saw this guy taking pictures in the middle of the street. I said to myself, "This guy is too close. It's too dangerous. He's risking his life. He has a telephoto lens — why is he so close to the bodies?" A few minutes after that, I said to myself, "I am stupid. When I came to cover this, I was as bad as he was. But when I saw the firemen running, I realized it was dangerous so I moved away."

WENDY DOREMUS | Widow of
Photojournalist William Biggart

NEW YORK: He was a portrait photographer all the way. It's frightening to see now how close he was.

> It's frightening to see now how close he was.

An image from William Biggart's final rolls of film. He was killed during the collapse of the North Tower, the only journalist to die covering the attacks.

William Biggart

9:40 A.M. CNN — FAA HALTS ALL FLIGHTS AT U.S. AIRPORTS.

9:42

9:43 A.M. AP NewsAlert: Washington — An aircraft has crashed into the Pentagon.

LISA BURGESS | Pentagon Reporter
Stars and Stripes

> It's not a stretch to think a major installation in Washington would be hit.

ARLINGTON, Va.: I was going down Corridor Seven and got as far as the central ring that overlooks the courtyard. Two janitors in front of me were pushing these huge gray carts, and two Army guys were running up my butt. I was thinking to myself that these guys should get out of the way. There were a lot more people in the courtyard because the weather was so nice.

I'm looking out the window, wishing I could get a cup of coffee. All of a sudden there was a very large noise, which reminded me of mortars except louder. It was followed by a second, slightly smaller explosion and vibration. The janitors in front of me fell over, and I kind of fell against the wall.

I wasn't scared at all. I'm a reporter. I pulled out my cell phone. I saw people running outside the window, and I could see they were screaming. A huge fireball was rising up kitty-corner to me. The two Army guys said, "What the hell was that?" I said, "We got hit." I knew instantly it was some kind of terrorist attack. This is a paranoid environment, but it's not a stretch to think a major installation in Washington would be hit.

The fireball was like a mini-mushroom cloud. The smoke was intense. It immediately rose up in the air and then dropped in the courtyard. The smoke just blotted out the sky.

STEPHEN LUCAS | Director
"Today in New York," WNBC News

NEW YORK: I looked up and saw our network feed from the Pentagon. It was up in flames and smoke. I informed the producer, and we let our talent know. We put that on the air. There was a sense of, "What's going on? Are we at war? What happened?" You just have that feeling of not knowing, but you're covering this event as it's happening. The whole sense of it is, "Where are we going with this?"

Corbin M. Harris/The Northern Virginia Journal

Smoke spews from the gaping hole in the Pentagon where a hijacked commercial jetliner slammed into the nation's military headquarters.

JOHN GREENWOOD | Photojournalist
| WRC

ARLINGTON, Va.: The assignment desk said to go to National Airport because it was going to affect travel all along the East Coast. So, we were traveling to the airport, and we were on Interstate 395, I'd say maybe two blocks from the Pentagon. You could see it. We heard a roar. It sounded like a large fist going into a large pillow, not like a bang. It was a "boom"! We looked to our left. An orange, flamey cloud was going up, and we knew something had hit the Pentagon.

We tried to get video. Of course, the authorities were trying to get us out of the area because they were trying to set up a perimeter. We finally got a live shot set, and we saw something that none of us will ever forget.

> ' The assignment desk said to go to National Airport because it was going to affect travel all along the East Coast. '

‘ Chet, you'd better put the Webcam on the Pentagon. I think something just exploded. ’

CRAIG COLA | Photographer
Washingtonpost.com

ARLINGTON, Va.: My boss, Chet Rhodes, told me to get to the airport and do a piece on the impending closing. I was driving down the George Washington Parkway and out of the corner of my eye I saw the Pentagon go up in flames. I was on the opposite side, so I didn't see the plane — just big, massive flames. I immediately called up Chet from my cell phone.

"Chet, you'd better put the Webcam on the Pentagon. I think something just exploded."

CHET RHODES | Senior Video Editor
Washingtonpost.com

ARLINGTON, Va.: Once I saw the second plane, I was in the terrorists' minds. If two planes, why not 10? I thought for sure that the White House would be next. (Staff photographer) Craig Cola called me minutes after the Pentagon (was hit) and shouted to turn the Webcam toward the Pentagon. On top of our building in Arlington we have a $3,000 camera. Minutes before, I had turned the Webcam toward the White House, just in case something hit it.

JOHN McWETHY, ARLINGTON, Va.: They were trying to funnel us into the courtyard. We didn't know what had happened. But we didn't want to be trapped in the courtyard if we were under attack. The outer doors are automatically locked, and the guards could not open the doors. They just punched through, and it set off alarms. At this point, we were outside in the parking lot, outside the mall entrance. Cars were on fire. It was an unbelievable scene of destruction, like Sarajevo and Somalia, where I've been.

All the cell lines were blocked. I kept dialing my desk. I would get through to New York, and someone would say, "Oh great! Thank God, you are alive. We are going to put you on the live line with Peter (Jennings)." Then they would lose me. I'd call back. They'd lose me.

I made my way to a Citgo (service) station and commandeered a land line. The whole network was in a crazy state. I have no sense of time. It felt like hours but was just minutes. I was speaking to the desk when some rent-a-cop came up to me and told me another plane was en route to hit the Pentagon. "You need to get out of here," he yelled. He made like he was going to pull a gun. So I said, "Look buddy, shoot me. I'm a reporter. I need to talk to my network."

> ' Look buddy, shoot me. I'm a reporter. I need to talk to my network. '

JOHN DEL GIORNO | Helicopter Reporter
Metro Networks/Shadow Broadcasting, WABC-TV

NEW YORK: At that point the focus of the story was that we had established this was a deliberate attack, that both planes crashing into both buildings is much more than a coincidence. The general feeling was that you were stunned. You were scared because you couldn't believe that it happened. But you knew it did because you would look out the window and see the buildings on fire. Then we hear that the Pentagon gets hit, and you say, "Well, what next?"

CHRISTINA PINO-MARINA | Reporter
Washingtonpost.com

ARLINGTON, Va.: It didn't occur to me to think something was coming this way. Not 10 minutes after the second plane hit, there was a huge explosion at the Pentagon. Everybody jumped out of their chairs and ran outside to the balcony. We are on the 11th floor and saw this huge cloud of smoke. It consumed the skyline. I called local police and fire contacts and couldn't get anybody. I finally got somebody in the Alexandria Fire Department, and they told me a gas station near the Pentagon was on fire.

My editor asked me to call the Airport Authority. They had not closed down yet. They were a wreck. They had trouble answering even simple questions.

MOLLY RILEY | News Assistant
Reuters

> I decided if I was going to get anywhere, I had to use my mountain bike.

ARLINGTON, Va.: I had been at the doctor's, got in my car at 9:50 a.m. and was listening to the radio. I called the desk and asked what was going on. Herman Beals, the senior photographer, said, "Everything short of World War III." He asked if I could go to the Pentagon and said, "Even if you can't get close, we at least need to show smoke." I carry a Nikon Coolpix with me. The digital quality is the same as any pool camera, but you can't change lenses.

By then the traffic was heavy. I decided if I was going to get anywhere, I had to use my mountain bike. I drove home. It wasn't that far. I parked, hopped on my bike with the Coolpix. I wasn't panicked. I was very focused. My first mission was to find the fastest way to get to the Pentagon.

Thick smoke billows from the Pentagon building in Arlington, Va., after it was struck by a hijacked airliner.

Molly Riley/Reuters

LISA BURGESS, ARLINGTON, Va.: We were not eager to evacuate. I knew that once we left the building, we wouldn't get back in. We walked out the doors into the courtyard. My plan was to try to figure out what had happened. I had no idea it was an aircraft that had crashed. Nobody knew.

Then more wounded people came out, and no one was there to help them. One guy who was bleeding profusely came staggering out. My colleague Sandra Jontz is an emergency medical technician. She immediately went to work on him, and I was running back and forth getting her scissors and bandages. She started cutting his clothes off. There were only about 15 people out there.

Then this other guy came staggering out, bleeding. I tried to help him. No sooner am I getting him to sit than the Pentagon police started yelling, "Evacuate the courtyard! There's another hijacked jet inbound!" Everybody just panicked. My stomach just turned over. There was no safety. Where could we go that it would be safe? We knew one side was gone. Where do you go?

Someone yelled, "False alarm!" so we headed back to the courtyard. The Pentagon police came again and said, "Evacuate! This is serious. They are tracking the aircraft, and you have six minutes until it's inbound. Get the hell out of here. You've got five minutes." We threw (together) whatever medical supplies we could that were scattered around the courtyard, and we headed into the building, figuring it was better than the empty courtyard. But no plane came.

> Evacuate the courtyard! There's another hijacked jet inbound!

CHARLES STROBLE | Chief Photographer
WBAL-TV

ARLINGTON, Va.: A bunch of old fellas, myself included, all said, "All right. Whew!" Took a deep breath and said, "Where are we going from here?" I've seen some stuff after 21 years, 22 years. This put me through a whole range of emotions that I never felt before in this business.

9:50 A.M. AP BULLETIN — WHITE HOUSE EVACUATED AFTER SECRET SERVICE RECEIVES THREAT.

EUGENIO HERNANDEZ | Assignment Manager/Producer
AP Television News

ARLINGTON, Va.: My shift didn't start until noon, so I was sleeping. I got a call from Spain from my mother around 8:55 a.m. As soon as she said there was a plane crashing into one of the towers, I hung up and called work. I threw on my pants and a shirt. I live in Alexandria (Va.). I got in my Jeep Cherokee and was driving on Interstate 395 toward D.C. and was listening to NPR. I saw the plane coming down like crazy. My first instinct after I saw the plane that low was, "Shit, this is related to New York."

When I saw the plane coming, I called one of my immediate supervisors, Gustavo Valcarcel, deputy editor of the Latin American desk. "Oh my God! A plane just hit the Pentagon. It's amazing. There's a lot of smoke." I was screaming. I was freaked out. My friend couldn't even understand who I was. "Who are you?" he asked. "Tell me again what you saw." I said, "I saw the plane coming like crazy. I'm here right now. Oh my God! You don't know what happened. A plane just hit the Pentagon. Oh my God!" They told me to calm down.

At that same moment, Dave Winslow had called in.

DAVE WINSLOW | Correspondent
The Associated Press

> I saw the tail go "whoosh," right past me. In an absolutely split second, you heard this loud boom.

ARLINGTON, Va.: I actually live in Pentagon City on the 10th floor of a 17-floor building that looks out at the city of Washington. I've got a wall of windows stretching from one side to the other. I hear this enormous sound of turbulence. I thought, "Oh my God, I know what's happening." You'd have to stand next to a plane on the runway to hear it that loud. I knew it was another attack.

As I turned to my right, I see a jumbo jet tail go by me along Interstate 395. It was like the rear end of the fuselage was riding on 395. I saw the tail go "whoosh," right past me. In an absolutely split second, you heard this loud boom.

JEFF RATHNER | Camera Operator
WETA

ARLINGTON, Va.: You just go on automatic pilot, do what you've always known as a photojournalist. You just start going and for 10 or 15 minutes, it's all happening. First, the helicopters are coming down, landing on the street, bodies out on the ground, people who are hurt. I didn't see any evidence of a plane. That was what was so startling. You could see the fire and smoke, but no fuselage. No nothing.

Your first instinct when they tell you to move back is to not listen to them. They usually run around and tell everybody and you usually wait until the second time they come around to tell you. But when they came by and they said there was another plane coming, well then you listen!

SONYA ROSS | White House Reporter
The Associated Press

ABOARD AIR FORCE ONE: There's a phone in the press cabin. It's used for urgent breaking news on a flight. It's something invoked very rarely. I'd only used it twice before — once when Air Force One hit some really bad turbulence with (President Bill) Clinton in 1996, and last year in garden-variety speculation about Hillary Clinton and the Senate race.

After takeoff, we were told that we were not going to D.C. but to an undisclosed location. They asked us not to use our cell phones and pagers because of the terrorists.

Once on the plane, everyone was checking in with their desks. We were hearing bits and snatches. Something about a car bomb at the State Department. I would say most people knew more than we did because we couldn't watch TV. I thought for a minute maybe I should refuse to go on the plane. Then I thought, "What kind of a punk am I? We go through all the routine and dullness for this kind of story." I just said to myself, "Duty calls and whatever will be, will be." I knew the plane was vulnerable. Yeah, it has special security, but it's still just an airplane.

> " I thought for a minute maybe I should refuse to go on the plane. "

ARSHAD MOHAMMED | White House Correspondent
Reuters

ABOARD AIR FORCE ONE: We get on the plane, and my notes say we took off at 9:54 a.m. Just before that, a White House official almost yelled — and people don't yell very much around here — "Is everybody on?" It did seem slightly panicky. We basically had no idea where we were going. The presumption was Washington, but we could tell over time that the plane had banked steeply and changed directions. The day before, we'd been able to see the beaches all the way down the coast. It was clear we were not flying up the Eastern Seaboard as we did the day before.

JOANNE LIPMAN | Weekend Journal Editor
The Wall Street Journal

NEW YORK: When we were trying to make our way out of there (near the World Trade Center), we heard on a radio that the Pentagon had been hit. As the crowd is making its way uptown, everyone was looking at landmarks. Everyone was watching the Empire State Building because you have no idea what might be coming next. Would there be more attacks?

EUGENIO HERNANDEZ, ARLINGTON, Va.: I didn't have a camera with me. On the left shoulder (of the road), I saw this tourist with a video camera. I got right behind the tourist, who was parked on the shoulder. The man was with his wife and son. They were from southern Virginia. He was freaked out completely.

He was not recording anything. The camera was facing the ground, basically. I jumped out of my car, pulled out one of my business cards and handed it to him. "I work for a news agency. Please could I borrow your camera?" At first, he refused. The guy says, "No, what's the AP?" I explained that this is a big news organization and I'm sure you will be rewarded if I can borrow your camera.

> I work for a news agency. Please could I borrow your camera?

He hands me the camera, and I went across the road inside the Pentagon area. No one stopped me. I was holding my press badge on top of my camera while I was recording; I walked as close as possible to the impact. There were people coming out of the Pentagon from both sides. There were police crews on the scene. Firetrucks were approaching.

The first firemen who got into the place where the plane crashed were just walking toward it. I was maybe 300 feet from the impact.

I recorded the people starting to put plastic sheets on the grass for the injured and preparing a triage area. There was a police patrol pulling blueprint maps out of the trunk to get the layout of the Pentagon. I recorded flames, people walking away. I didn't see anybody running; it was very calm. I got about five to eight minutes' worth. The guy had video from another vacation, and I recorded on top of that.

Later, I was thinking, "God, I was crazy to go so close."

> I recorded the people starting to put plastic sheets on the grass for the injured and preparing a triage area.

Rescue workers set up a triage area in the courtyard of the Pentagon, tending to the injured.

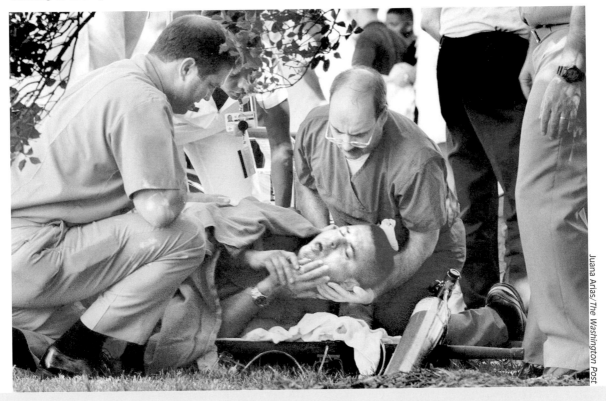

Juana Arias/*The Washington Post*

10:06

10:07 A.M. **AP FLASH: NEW YORK — ONE WORLD TRADE CENTER TOWER COLLAPSES.**

LIVE
E D T

WORLD TRADE CENTER
NEW YORK CITY

NBC NEWS

SPECIAL REPORT: ATTACK ON AMERICA

Matt Lauer: *"Let's go back — we just saw a live picture of what seemed to be a portion of the building falling away from the World Trade Center. I don't know whether it's another explosion or a portion of the building falling away, but something major just happened to that building."*

LINGLING SUN | **General Manager**
China Daily Distribution Corp.

NEW YORK: The first tower collapsed right in front of my eyes. I was across the street. It was like a slow-motion movie. The building looked like it was a candle melting. Nobody believed it. Everybody was looking at each other saying, "What is happening?" There was a big burst of crying from people, then there was smoke.

MARY GAY TAYLOR | **City Hall Reporter**
WCBS 880

NEW YORK: It came down like dominoes. I started to run and realized I could not outrun it, so I got under the back bumper of an ambulance. I'd spoken to a friend of mine earlier who works for the (New York) *Daily News.* He had dropped his child at day care (near the World Trade Center) and saw a guy next to him get killed by something falling. Bearing that in mind, I got under the bumper. Then it started coming down, and my face was covered with stuff. I couldn't breathe. I thought I might be buried alive.

> I couldn't breathe. I thought I might be buried alive.

Susan Watts/New York Daily News

Photographer Susan Watts' shot of crowds fleeing from the World Trade Center area.

SUSAN WATTS | Staff Photographer
(New York) Daily News

> I dive under a truck, my lenses are flying out of my pouch.

NEW YORK: Suddenly I felt something like an earthquake. I heard the police screaming, "Run! Run!" I turned back around, and everything was happening in slow motion. I see this billowing tornado coming down the street right at me. There was a fraction of a second in my mind where my instinct was to lift the camera, but then I thought, "Shit, I'd better run." I'm running, realizing this thing is going to kill me when it hits me.

I think it's a bomb. I'm running and it's like a stampede — like a cartoon — "Run for your lives!" I dive under a truck, my lenses are flying out of my pouch, my flash rips off the hot shoe. I see in my head what I think is a bomb hit the truck and explode on top of me. So I get out and run into a pharmacy. I look back outside and it's black as night.

Everyone starts screaming "It's a bomb! The windows are going to shatter." I run to the back of the pharmacy and pick up the phone because none of the cells are working. I call my editor. "None of us are safe! I'm trapped. We're all going to die." I was really thinking, this is the day I'm going to die.

I was too close. I never thought you could ever be too close. Moments before the building fell, cops had been pushing the photographers back. I argued with them saying, "You can't push us back! You're censoring us. This story is too big." But (a policeman) said, "If you don't move back, I'm going to arrest you." You know what? The guy was right, and who knew?

JOHN BUSSEY | **Foreign Editor**
The Wall Street Journal

NEW YORK: I heard this metallic roar, looked up and saw what I thought was just a very peculiar sight of individual floors, one after the other exploding outward. I thought to myself, "My God, they're going to bring the building down." And they, whoever they are, had set charges. In fact, the building was imploding down.

I saw the explosions, and I thought, "This is not a good place to be, because we're too close to the building, and it's too easy for the building to topple over." So I went under the desk in the office where I sought shelter. What shattered across the street broke the windows and came into the office where I was. It was all the detritus of the South Tower collapsing and spilling like an avalanche across the street.

I was under the desk in total pitch-black, completely thick air. I yanked my shirt off and put it over my face to keep the big stuff out. I was feeling my way around the office until I found my way out. Like so many modern offices, it has cubicles and partitions and dividers, and I got completely disoriented. I was stuck in this area. By accident, I felt my way out of it. As soon as I was out, I went down an emergency exit and out on the street where it was almost as bad. The emergency and rescue teams were looking for each other, looking for their colleagues because they got swept away.

It was a surreal environment, very peaceful. There was no sound. The other tower was still burning a couple blocks away. Ash was falling, two, three, four inches deep on everything and on people.

> ' Emergency and rescue teams were ... looking for their colleagues, because they got swept away. '

CATHERINE LEUTHOLD | **Photographer**
Free-lance

> ' I thought we were in nuclear war. '

NEW YORK: It took everything for me to get there that morning. I saw the first plane hit on TV before 9 a.m., then grabbed my cameras and ran to the subway. I remember shaking on the subway and then running down Broadway. I couldn't understand why both towers were burning because I had been in the subway when the second plane hit. I stopped in front of St. Paul's Chapel and must have taken about five pictures when all of a sudden the South Tower started collapsing in front of me. The sound was this deep, deep rumbling roar, like a jet taking off. There were a few screams. I felt so alone. There wasn't a single person around me. And then came silence and the cloud.

I put my shirt over my mouth and closed my eyes to protect them. I remember thinking I wasn't going to live but I was still living. I think about those people who didn't survive. How long were they alive for?

At this point, I thought we were in nuclear war. I'm talking out loud, saying over and over, "My name is Catherine Leuthold. I'm a photographer. Can anyone hear me?" A Spanish-speaking man all of a sudden wrapped his arms around me. I could feel he had stuff all over him. I can't

10:11 A.M. AP — WITNESSES REPORT SEEING PEOPLE FALLING AND JUMPING FROM TOWERS.

remember his name for the life of me. We hear, "Over here. There's a door."

This man, my angel, pulled us in. People were hunched down by the water cooler. I wiped my lens and started taking pictures of these people at the water cooler. I went into the bathroom and I looked in the mirror. I was this person with white ash all over. I was having trouble breathing.

It was about 10:10 a.m. and I went out and found Major Reginald Mebane, a New York court officer. I was in shock. I was on autopilot. I remember seeing his face and thinking, "He's reflecting my face." I just saw these eyes looking at me and to me they just captured what it was. He was in shock. He didn't say anything to me. We both kind of looked at each other. I said, "Are you all right?"

I was thinking of the people and their faces. This really wasn't happening. It was so quiet. I was just telling myself to take pictures, take pictures. He was just standing there, right after he escaped from the South Tower as it collapsed. I think I asked him, "Is it all right if I take your picture? I took a series of four, and this is the last one. I know I was talking to him because he's looking right at me. There was just this moment when we both understood.

Catherine Leuthold's images from the fallen towers and the aftermath, including a self-portrait (far left), and New York court officer Reginald Mebane (far right), who helped with rescue efforts.
Photos by Catherine Leuthold

Ruth Fremson/The New York Times

Ruth Fremson's shot of an ash-covered police officer, leaning against a case in the Stage Door Deli in Lower Manhattan.

RUTH FREMSON | Staff Photographer
The New York Times

> **Stay calm,
> keep working.**

NEW YORK: I was pointing my camera up at the top of the building, waiting to see a third plane. Instead, I started seeing the metal panels popping off the building, like popcorn. I thought, "Stay calm, keep working." Then I saw police and firemen running, and I started running. I could feel this tidal wave behind me. I saw this man in a white shirt roll under this vehicle, and I just rolled under it with him. I just clutched his arm or leg. I still don't know what part of his body I gave a bruise to.

I opened my eyes. I couldn't see anything. Every breath was scratchy. But I realized I was breathing. I was getting oxygen. I realized I was still alive. I said hello to the guy next to me. I said, "I'm Ruth Fremson from *The New York Times*. He says, "Hi, I'm Dan Mullin. I'm a cop." We were both totally calm and having a conversation like we'd just met in a bar. As things began to settle, we heard glass breaking. We hear, "Hello, hello, hello." I thought, "Somebody needs help, and we can't even see them."

They were inside the deli across the sidewalk. Dan and I stumbled in, and there was a handful of people in there. I cleaned off my cameras and washed my face. There was a phone in the deli. I was able to call the desk, tell them I was down there, that the first building was down, and I would go back out as soon as the smoke cleared.

I started making some pictures. I realized it was just as important what was happening inside the deli as outside. I made the picture of the cop.

BETH FERTIG | Reporter
WNYC Radio

NEW YORK: I was about to cross Broadway at the traffic circle when this big female cop says, "I can't let you go any farther." I showed my press pass and mike. She says, "I'm doing this to save your life" and, on cue, the building came down. I just held out my mike and let it roll on my minidisc. I got the sound of the rumble, like having a giant elevated train over your head. It was just unbelievable to see this 110-story tower coming down perfectly. I start narrating on the mike what I'm seeing. Then this giant cloud of smoke with debris starts pouring east, sucked through the canyons of Lower Manhattan. I started running north. All these people were screaming and running, like a Godzilla movie.

> ' I'm doing this to save your life. '

CAROL MARIN | Contributor
CBS News

NEW YORK: I was frantically punching my cell phone and one of the things I hit was my Chicago producer's number. I told them I was on my way to the World Trade Center. As I said that, the first collapse of the tower happened. I was on the line and said, "Oh my God, there's been an explosion." I still had not processed that a whole building was down. I kept walking. As they were cautioning me to be careful, the line went dead.

10:13 A.M. CNN — THE UNITED NATIONS BUILDING EVACUATES.

BOLÍVAR ARELLANO | Photographer
New York Post

> ❝ That's it. I hope somebody finds my camera because I'm going to be dead. ❞

NEW YORK: A Latino cop saw me hiding behind the fence and threw me out. He pushed me three times on my back and told me to get out because the building was coming down. I said, "No, it won't. Remember (the) 1993 (attack). It's going to be fine." He took me one block away from the building. Then he had to come back to push others out of the way, so I came back again. The building was in front of me but I turned my back. Then I hear the explosion. I saw the top of the building coming down. I took one frame, and thought, "That's it. I hope somebody finds my camera because I'm going to be dead."

In front of me was a man kneeling, looking at the building coming down. I said to myself, "I'm going to die anyway, so let me see if I can save his life." I jumped on his back, embraced his stomach and held tight to a piece of rail near me, so when the building comes down we don't fly. The building came down with the debris. Thank God, nothing happened to us. The man was covered with dust like me, and his eyes were open with surprise. Later I learned he was Thomas Manley, sergeant-at-arms for the Uniformed Firefighters Association.

Bolívar Arellano captures the South Tower's collapse. He took one shot and then was caught in the falling debris.

Bolívar Arellano/New York Post

MARTY GLEMBOTZKY | **Photographer**
WABC-TV

NEW YORK: (WABC-TV reporter N.J. Burkett) said he wanted to do a stand-up. He motioned, "Me, the firefighters and tilt up to the building." I asked for another one (a second take), as I always do, because you never know, there could be a crease in the tape or whatever. As I tilted up, the density of sound in the area changed. It became thick. As I tilted up, I could feel it, but I couldn't really tell you that I knew what I was seeing. I was seeing the building blow up.

I kept tilting up and heard him (Burkett) say that the building was exploding. I heard him scream that we'd better get out of the way. I heard him run. I opened my left eye and saw two firefighters running. I looked in the viewfinder again and realized that I was in the debris field. This was a large building, and I was going to be crushed.

I looked back. There were three revolving doors behind me, and firefighters were getting caught in them. They were locked. At the end, there was an open door. I mean, this is at the point of fight or flight. Two firefighters fell. I ran. I jumped over them. I had the camera with me, but I do not remember whether I was rolling it or not.

I was not at work anymore. I was running for my life. It was absolutely the worst feeling ever. I went in that doorway. We ran into the Winter Garden, which is an all-glass atrium. All at once there were five of us. I felt people pull me back. Our backs were up against a phone bank, and we heard the building come down.

> ❛ I was not at work anymore. I was running for my life. ❜

PAUL STEIGER | **Managing Editor**
The Wall Street Journal

NEW YORK: I started working my way around the boat basin toward the esplanade that goes along the Hudson River, looking for more *Journal* staffers. All of a sudden, down comes the tower. I felt like someone in Pompeii when Vesuvius erupted. Instantly, we were surrounded by a choking cloud of debris.

TOM FLYNN | Producer
CBS News

NEW YORK: I raced to a parking garage along with rescue workers who all had walkie-talkies. A half dozen of us went into a parking garage on Battery Street, toward the river. The lights went out. We were on the ground floor. The dust roared in like a huge tsunami of hot wind, sand, heat. It filled up the garage. I had a death grip on (my) bike. I felt like that was going to get me out alive. I just had this vision of getting to the river and riding up to CBS. I had it all planned — me and the bike. One guy said, "I think I'd leave that bike behind if I were you." So polite in the middle of Armageddon.

We got out. The streetlights came on because it was dark. People were calm. People were in the river. I don't know if they were blown in or jumped.

> ' I just had this vision of getting to the river and riding up to CBS. ,

SARA KUGLER | Writer
The Associated Press

NEW YORK: Our little group ran into 20 Vesey Street. By then, I wasn't in the quote mode. I felt a lot better having a police officer with us, although he seemed scared. As the smoke and dust came right in, it became difficult to breathe. That was scary. The officer decided we needed to be lower and directed us down a rickety staircase, with no lights, along this long, winding hall to a room where we found a fan. I was wearing sandals with a one-and-a-half-inch heel. My shoe got caught on the stairs. I jiggled it free and then it got caught on the next one, but I didn't want to go barefoot.

In the room, there was a phone that worked, and the officer made a call. At one point, he hung up and left the room to check upstairs. So I picked up the phone to call the AP. He came back in and yelled, "What are you doing?" I told him, "I'm a reporter and I was just going to call my office." He yelled at me, "F--- your job." So I hung up.

Gulnara Samoilova/The Associated Press

Gulnara Samoilova's photograph of people covered with dust as they walk away from the attack site.

GULNARA SAMOILOVA | Photo Retouch Artist
The Associated Press

NEW YORK: I hear this terrible noise and lift my camera up — I had the 80 mm portrait lens on. I shoot this photo while the building is collapsing. Everybody is running and I fell. I thought, "This is it." I thought people were going to run over me. I was able to get up. I'm looking back and this huge cloud is coming toward me — I mean, tremendous! I think I'm not going to make it. I sit down behind a car, and this very strong wind comes with all this debris and dust and smoke. Then it was totally dark. Everything goes into my eyes, ears and nose. I'm sitting there in the total dark. I'm thinking I'm buried alive. I start choking because there's no air to breathe. Then it was total silence. I can hear the papers flying. That's what I remember — papers flying in the air and it's dark.

I got up and started shooting again. People were walking around in a daze, including me. I took a picture of a large group of people walking. They're covered in dust, and you can't really see if they are black or white. There is terror in their eyes. I felt like I was one of them.

> I hear this terrible noise and lift my camera up.

10:16

SUZANNE PLUNKETT | Photographer
The Associated Press

> ' Your dad called. He's a wreck. '

NEW YORK: I crossed Broadway to start arguing with a cop about getting access when I heard someone say, "They're coming down! Run for your life!" Everyone started running toward me, and I saw a billowing cloud of debris like "The Blob" coming down the street. I was leaning on an SUV behind me, and all these people had to go by me. It was very lucky I had set my cameras on auto while I was in the subway. I just had the shutter going. The shot of people fleeing was frame 14.

A cop told me I had to go. I remember running for my life and thinking, "This is it." I remember feeling like I was so fatigued, like a dream, like I was running through jam. I ran for a short distance and a cloud went over me. You can't see anything. It's dark and I couldn't breathe. It was very silent. I ran

Suzanne Plunkett's photograph of people fleeing the collapse of the second tower and the cloud of dust that poured down the street.

Suzanne Plunkett/The Associated Press

10:11

into an alley to hide under a car because I was thinking the building was going to fall on me. I was crouched in an alley and called my dad in Minnesota and left a message on his answering machine, "Don't worry, I'm safe, I'll be OK." But I was crying. I knew I had that first shot (people fleeing) and had to get it out, so I found a vitamin shop and asked to use their outlet to plug in my computer. You take your disk from the camera and put it in your laptop to view and choose, then you work in Photoshop to put your caption on. I got a phone line, and sent three to AP. Joan (Rosen, New York state photo editor for AP) told me to go to one of our editor's ex-roommate's apartment, which they began to use as a base. I asked if she got the pictures, and she said, "Your dad called. He's a wreck."

ROBERT J. HUGHES | Reporter
The Wall Street Journal

NEW YORK: From the street level, it was like an avalanche. I was standing about 100 yards from Tower Two. It was collapsing out toward us. I forced my way into a lobby at 130 Broadway. It was filling up quickly with smoke and soot, and people were screaming and crying. The doors suddenly shut behind us, and we were trapped. We thought we were going to suffocate. We found our way into an open door downstairs. But when we got through, the door closed behind us and locked. It was the entrance to the Wall Street subway station. There were about 100 people. One woman had an asthma attack, and people were shouting at each other to calm down. We were all standing there holding shirts over our noses in a 20-by-40-foot space.

There was a rescue worker who had run with us. He managed to force open another door to an adjacent building, and we walked through several passageways to another building with windows to the street. We saw ghostly figures going by through the ash. Finally, we found a crowbar and were able to pry open a door and escape to the street. It was like a ghost world outside.

> We were all standing there holding shirts over our noses in a 20-by-40-foot space.

PATRICK WITTY | **Photographer**
Free-lance

NEW YORK: As I was walking closer to (the burning towers) all these people were looking up. I turned around and shot a picture, just at the exact second the first tower was coming down (see page 56). You can see on my film that the next frame was blurred as I swung to the right to turn around, and the next picture was the smoke. I was probably five blocks away. All the people (in the picture) just took off running.

As it started to come down, I started to walk closer. A huge wall of dust and debris started coming toward us. I shot two or three pictures and just started running. Everyone who was young and relatively strong just started grabbing people. It was a completely instinctive situation. A lot of people seemed to be in shock. We beat it out of there just as the first wave of ash descended.

> People seemed to be in shock. We beat it out of there just as the first wave of ash descended.

HERNANDO REYES SMIEKER | **Reporter**
Noticias 1380

NEW YORK: We see the building start to collapse, so we start to run. The guy I was interviewing was running right behind me. We reach a cop who says, "Get down! Get down to the floor!" I see him getting under a station wagon. We follow the fire workers, and we get under the car. We see a big black cloud and then nothing. That moment is so long for us. There are four people under the car and we are talking together. I notice my tape recorder is on, taping the conversation. The policeman asks me, "What's your name?" We are asking each other, "How do you feel?" It starts to clear. We can see more, and I can breathe. I have a lot of dust in my mouth and I try to spit it out, but I can't. I try to reach my radio station, but the cell phone is not working. I get inside one of the buildings and ask for a telephone. I made my report. I was live on the air. Don't ask me how I did it.

Shannon Stapleton/Reuters

Shannon Stapleton's photograph of rescue workers carrying the body of the Rev. Mychal Judge from the rubble. Judge was the chaplain for the New York fire department.

SHANNON STAPLETON | Photographer
Free-lance

NEW YORK: When the first tower went down, I was about four blocks away, so I hightailed it out of there and ran as fast as I could down a side street. These people who were in a restaurant pulled me in, and everyone went under a table. You could feel stuff hitting the sides of the building.

I ran back outside and got down right around the base of the Trade Center. That's when I made the image of Father (Mychal) Judge (chaplain for the New York fire department) being carried out. It was just me and (photographer) James Nachtwey. It was really strange how it happened. I noticed (rescue workers) carrying this man in a chair. I knew it was a pretty intense image. They weren't too happy. I made those frames and started getting away from the perimeter.

I did not know that it was Father Judge until three days later. I heard that he was giving last rites and supposedly a body fell on him and killed him. I kept seeing his face. I was having a lot of trouble with that — just seeing his face and hearing the sirens.

'I knew it was a pretty intense image.'

New York *Daily News* photographer David Handschuh is carried to safety after his leg was broken while he was shooting the collapse of the World Trade Center.

DAVID HANDSCHUH | Photographer
(New York) Daily News

> Just run,
> just run.

NEW YORK: I'm across the street from the South Tower when, all of a sudden, it collapses. It starts to disintegrate, piece by piece. I started to bring my camera up to my eyes, but something said to me, "Just run, just run." I've never, ever, run away from an assignment in more than 20 years of doing this, but running from that saved my life. If I had continued to take pictures, I would have been killed. The fire department chaplain (Mychal Judge) who was killed was probably no more than 50 feet from where I was standing when he was killed.

I looked over my shoulder and saw a wall of debris flying in my direction — bricks, rock, water, glass. It was almost like the approach of a tornado. As I was running, I wound up underneath some kind of motor vehicle. It was dark and hot, almost like being hit by a wave of gravel. It had a thick, thick consistency. I banged my head on the bumper of the car. But I was alive. I tried moving and knew that my leg was broken. I was trapped. I started screaming for help. I don't know how long it was until a group of firemen dug through the rubble, pulled me out and carried me to a nearby delicatessen.

TODD MAISEL | Photographer
(New York) Daily News

NEW YORK: I dived into a building lobby, rolling and striking a wall as I came to a rest in a fetal position. Walls and ceilings exploded. Debris rained from everywhere. The lobby fell dark and I could barely breathe. Was this going to be my tomb? I began crawling out (of the building lobby) backward the same way I believed I came from. The street was littered with overturned ambulances, emergency vehicles burning.

A firefighter stood among the burning trucks, a water can in his hand, gazing up at the sky blankly. I began going from ambulance to firetruck, looking for injured. I could hear a voice calling for help. I came upon a medic with a partially covered firefighter. We pushed the semiconscious firefighter on to a backboard and carried him with rescuers at least two blocks, where we found the fire surgeon (though injured, he survived).

Then I found fellow photographer David Handschuh of the (New York) *Daily News*, his leg broken in three places. A cop and two firefighters carried him, and I took his cameras.

' Was this going to be my tomb? '

New York *Daily News* photographer Todd Maisel (in red helmet) and firefighters carry Armando Reno, chauffeur of Engine 65, from debris.

Robert Mecea

STAN HONDA | **Photo Stringer**
Agence France-Presse

NEW YORK: As the dust cloud came toward us, a policeman pulled people into the lobby of a bank building. I went inside, and half a minute later this woman comes in who was completely covered with the dust and debris. It was such a strange sight. It was difficult to see what she was wearing. She seemed pretty stunned. I took only one photo. There's a lot of detail in the picture — you see a necklace, some jewelry, and you actually see a face staring at you. That seems to make a human connection with this kind of unfathomable tragedy. The woman asked to be taken to a hospital, and a police officer helped her to an upper floor.

I went outside and began photographing what was happening with police and rescue workers. I got this photo of a businessman who was walking out of the debris. I realized he was still carrying his briefcase amid all this chaos. Here's a guy trying to walk out of this disaster with his suit intact, clutching his briefcase.

> **She seemed pretty stunned. I took only one photo.**

Stan Honda photographed people after one of the towers collapsed. At right, a woman is covered with dust. Below, a businessman tries to breathe through his handkerchief.

Photos by Stan Honda/Agence France-Presse

PAUL STEIGER, NEW YORK: A couple thousand people tried to make their way along the river to escape that cloud. But the wind was blowing south, so the cloud stayed with us. Some people jumped in the water or fell into the water, but that didn't do them any good because the cloud came right down on top of the water.

There were babies in carriages, there were dogs, there were nannies, there were people carrying their briefcases. There were all manner of folk. Everybody that I could see was acting in a totally socially positive way, helping each other, warning each other to shield their noses, helping people lift strollers over steps. I had a brand-new tie that my son had given me for my birthday, and I wrapped it around my nose. We passed the Holocaust Memorial and got down to South Ferry, which was as far as we could go. We were still surrounded by this choking cloud, but after 10 or 15 minutes, it dissipated, and we could breathe again.

JIM PENSIERO | Assistant Managing Editor
The Wall Street Journal

NEW YORK: The ferries were running; they just waved every-body on. I took the boat to Jersey City. We were on the other side when the South Tower fell. It was like a volcano, a tremen-dous roar. You're seeing it from a mile away, but it's a straight shot — something out of Dante. I was watching thousands of lives being snuffed out and I knew it.

Some people on the ferry cried. There were some people still trying to reschedule meetings. I think they didn't really get it until they saw that happen. I knew that when both tow-ers were hit that it was an extraordinary story. I knew it was off the charts when I witnessed the South Tower fall. That's when I said, "I've witnessed a mass murder here." I didn't know at that point when it was going to stop. It really felt like we were at war. At that point it was, "Well, I still have my assignment; I'd better keep going."

> ' I've witnessed a mass murder here. '

ARIS ECONOMOPOULOS | Staff Photographer
The Star-Ledger,
Newark, N.J.

> I went right to Ground Zero. I had to see what had happened.

NEW YORK: In complete darkness, I climb up the (subway) steps, using my hands to feel my way up the handrail. Now I'm back on the street where you can see maybe two inches in front of you. I see this light coming at me. It's a glass door with light coming through. I go inside and am all by myself, when I hear voices outside. I open the door into this thick smoke and shout to them to come to my voice. A half-dozen people come in. It's a real emotional scene with people crying and hugging. One lady is freaking out, yelling, "Oh my God, we're alive!"

I'm a photographer and don't give myself time emotionally to feel what is happening because I have a job to do. I try to clean off my (camera) lenses and start taking pictures (right). One of the two ladies in the picture was the one who is screaming, "Oh my God, I'm alive!" The one on the left asked me why I was taking pictures. I said, "We have to remember this. We cannot forget."

I started photographing a group of NYPD officers trying to wash ash out of their eyes. They were definitely rattled. There was one guy, about six feet five inches, football-linebacker size, and the bridge of his nose was cut and dusty. The only thing he could say was, "This is war. This is war."

After that — probably not the smartest idea — but I went right to Ground Zero. I had to see what had happened. I walked right to what was the South Tower. It felt like the twilight zone. A guy asked me to take his photo with a disposable point-and-shoot (camera) in front of the wreckage, but I could not do it. I had a film camera with me and started getting low on film. There were only a couple of photographers there — me, (James) Nachtwey and a few others, plus cops and firefighters. It was bedlam in the sense that I'm used to being told to get the hell out of there, but I was their least concern. I bumped into Don Halasy of the *New York Post* and asked if he could spare a roll of film. He gave me one of his only two or three rolls left. He said, "Shoot smart!"

Photos by Aris Economopoulos/The Star-Ledger, Newark, N.J.

Aris Economopoulos took these photographs of shaken survivors (top) and police officers cleaning ash from their eyes (bottom).

> I let go of my tape recorder to clear stuff off my face.

MARY GAY TAYLOR, NEW YORK: I let go of my tape recorder to clear stuff off my face and backed out from under the bumper. I couldn't see anything. It was pitch-black. I backed out farther and stood up and still couldn't see. I was so disoriented. Did something happen to my eyes? Am I blind? Am I buried?

I said, "Why can't I see?" No one said anything. Off to my right I saw a flashlight and a man in a helmet from EMS (Emergency Medical Service). Oh my goodness, he was like my savior. Then I realized we were in this black cloud. It began to lift and got lighter.

MARTY GLEMBOTZKY, NEW YORK: We found a construction trailer, went inside and called our wives. It was a brutal conversation. My wife was hysterical. So was his (N.J. Burkett). We called the desk. Then we had to go back to the story.

The woman in the trailer told me she saw the first plane hit. I said, "We have to interview this woman." She did not want to do it. We worked her for 10 minutes.

We went outside and started interviewing this woman. I very selfishly got low on my knees and shot straight up because I knew that the fire was still burning in the North Tower, and the South Tower was gone.

This was the piece of a lifetime, and I knew it. She was a great interview. She witnessed it. She was crying. It was brutal. We were crying while interviewing her, listening to her talk.

BETSY STEUART CUNNINGHAM | Producer
NBC News

WASHINGTON: There is a system of squawk boxes installed around the State Department that normally alert you to a fire drill or evacuation. That system said,"There's a fire in the State Department. Move to an exit." We said, "What the hell is that about?" I started making phone calls. Then the message turned into, "This is an evacuation, you must evacuate the building immediately." I called my office and said we were being ordered to evacuate the building, and they said, "Get out, but take your cell phone."

I went outside and the deputy assistant secretary of state for the Middle East was standing in front of the building like everyone else. I asked him if anyone had claimed responsibility. He didn't think so, but said, "I bet we know who did it."

It was decided that the State Department press operation was going to move to the Foreign Press Center in the National Press Building. Several colleagues and I decided to walk there.

I got beeped by my office. There was a report that a car bomb had gone off at the State Department. I said, "There is no car bomb." They wanted me to walk around the building, so I did. I told them, "I promise you, there is no car bomb here." It took about 15 minutes to make sure that a note telling people that there was no car bomb was put into what we call the hot file — a file in our computer system where we put information we want everyone to know. I later learned that Tom Brokaw went on the air and said that "Betsy Steuart, our reporter at the State Department, assured us there was no car bomb."

' I promise you, there is no car bomb here. '

BARBARA WOIKE | **Photo Editor**
NYC Bureau, The Associated Press

NEW YORK: When the tower collapsed, we were worried about our photographers. We were getting calls from their family members, but we couldn't reach them because the cells weren't working. We tried different cell phones with different services, but nothing worked. Then we had transmission problems. Did we want the photographers to leave the scene to come back to our office? The subways weren't working, and we couldn't send a messenger to them. It was a real dilemma. How would we get their pictures? My old roommate has an apartment at 310 Greenwich, and we decided to send photographers to her apartment to transmit, until she lost power.

Carolina Salguero/SIPA Press

The offices of *The Wall Street Journal* near the World Trade Center were covered in dust and debris.

JOANNE LIPMAN | Weekend Journal Editor
The Wall Street Journal

NEW YORK: We were able to walk up along the water to our design director's apartment in SoHo. The tower collapsed just as we were getting there. We then tried to locate people on the cell, trying to get phone calls out. That was one of the most frightening things. I ultimately was able to get through to my family but had a very hard time finding some of my colleagues. I will tell you that there was a lot of fear. We knew that (managing editor) Paul Steiger had put several people on the ferry to get them to New Jersey, but no one was able to reach Paul. We were really frightened about that.

SAM BOYLE | New York City Bureau Chief
The Associated Press

' Communications were hellacious. '

NEW YORK: Communications were hellacious. We were constantly calling cell phones, hoping to get an answer. You dial and dial and dial, and maybe it would go through. It's foreign to our experience to imagine the southern part of Manhattan gone. Pay phones were not working. You could not get in touch with anyone south of 14th Street.

10:26 A.M. CNN — ALL INBOUND TRANSATLANTIC FLIGHTS ARE DIVERTED TO CANADA.

MAGGIE FARLEY | **Bureau Chief, U.N./Canada**
Los Angeles Times

NEW YORK: Being eight months pregnant, I was already in comfortable shoes. When I went out the door, I didn't know at that point that the building had fallen. My husband (Marcus Brauchli, national news editor of *The Wall Street Journal*) was on the Brooklyn Bridge and saw the tower fall. I was walking toward the bridge and Marcus and another editor were walking back. They decided they'd be most useful back (in Brooklyn) trying to make phone calls, locate people. He looked at me and said, "Don't even try. I don't want you to go."

But I felt like I had to try. I went to the (Brooklyn) bridge, and there were thousands of people coming across like a parade of refugees. Suddenly the stream of people turned into a throng that looked like the "Night of the Living Dead." I tried to find people who were coherent enough to interview. At the beginning a lot of people were so shaky, they were crying. They didn't want their names used.

Though I had a police pass, the police wouldn't let me get on the bridge because so many people were coming from New York City to Brooklyn. But I was in the reporter mode, and I felt this journalistic desperation to get to the scene. I felt this weird sort of guilt that I wasn't able to get there that day.

> ' I felt this journalistic desperation to get to the scene. '

HAROLD DOW | **Correspondent**
"48 Hours," CBS News

NEW YORK: I hear this freight train, look up and this thing is coming down. I was on a street filled with shoes. People had literally run out of their shoes. Normally, I would never go into a subway in a case like this, but I figured if I got hit with something, I'm dead.

I ran into a subway station, and three or four people ran in with me. We ran into a shoe place. I asked if I could use the phone. I called Dan (Rather) and he put me live on the air.

10:28

10:29 A.M. AP FLASH: New York — Second World Trade Center tower collapses.

CNN LIVE — BREAKING NEWS

AMERICA UNDER ATTACK

Aaron Brown (live at 10:28 a.m.): *"The trade centers here in New York have been hit by airplanes. In Washington, there is a large fire at the Pentagon. The Pentagon has been evacuated. And, there as you can see, perhaps the second tower, the front tower, the top portion of which is collapsing. Good Lord. There are no words."*

SAM BOYLE | New York City Bureau Chief
The Associated Press

NEW YORK: One thing I've never seen in my experience of 30 years with the AP is running two "flashes" within a half-hour. Flash is a news alert. It's a signal that a story is of the utmost importance and is only to be used in extreme situations. We wouldn't use flash to announce a presidential election. I've never used flash before myself.

MARTY GLEMBOTZKY | Photographer
WABC-TV

NEW YORK: People started running. We heard someone say that the tower was leaning. (WABC-TV reporter N.J. Burkett) yelled, "This is our story! Start rolling!" I am walking backward. Then he said we had better get out of the way. It was a judgment call on my part. I tilted up, and held for as long as I felt safe. Then I ran for my life.

You do what you have to do. As a photographer, you want to illustrate the story visually. I felt it was important to try to capture as much as possible. That is your job. It is not always the smartest thing, because you can get killed.

> People started running. We heard someone say that the tower was leaning.

10:30 A.M. AP — NEW YORK GOV. GEORGE PATAKI DECLARES STATE OF EMERGENCY.

SONYA ROSS | White House Reporter
The Associated Press

> ‘ A camera caught the image of me bringing my hands to cover my face. ’

ABOARD AIR FORCE ONE: Ann Compton (of ABC News) and I are talking over the seats and synchronizing watches to do a timeline. We thought from here on out we should keep note of everything that happens and what time. I was making notes and listening to the TV on a headset. A reporter on the TV, I don't remember what network it was, started yelling, "Now the second tower is collapsing."

I looked up. Just as I did, a camera caught the image of me bringing my hands to cover my face as I watched the tower

Aboard Air Force One, Associated Press White House reporter Sonya Ross watches a TV monitor showing the collapse of the North Tower of the World Trade Center. Behind her is ABC News correspondent Ann Compton.

Khue Bui for Newsweek

10:31

falling. In the back of my mind, I was thinking that thousands have to be dead. I noticed that nobody on TV was even speculating on the death toll. I was just mortified. I'd never seen anything like it. Not even in the worst action movie in the world.

Here we are in the air with no idea where we are going, and I was trying not to think of some surface-to-air missile hitting us. When the tower collapsed we all just looked at each other. A ripple of "Oh my God!" went through the plane. Nobody was really saying much. Right after that our signal started to fade, and the picture got all snowy.

Some of my colleagues came up after that picture appeared and said, "You really conveyed what we all felt." At first I was embarrassed. I didn't want to look like I wasn't doing my job. But how can you report the emotions of others if you are not in touch with your own feelings and thoughts?

> How can you report the emotions of others if you are not in touch with your own feelings and thoughts?

KHUE BUI | Contributing Photographer
Newsweek

ABOARD AIR FORCE ONE: At this point, none of us had seen the actual plane crash into the World Trade Center. People on Air Force One arranged for us to hook up with a local TV station so we could see what was going on. I was looking for something to take pictures of. The Secret Service guys came back to watch our TV. (There are separate cabins on Air Force One where they were seated.) I was trying to get a reaction off a Secret Service man's face, but they are stoic. They don't show a lot.

Our cabin has a TV at the very front. Sonya (Ross) was in the second row back. I was crouched in the press cabin. I was looking for any kind of moment, since everything was happening in New York City. We can't roam around the plane, so I was trying to get something documented. Then I shot Sonya's face. I shot a photo of the Reuters writer, Arshad Mohammed, too. It's got a time stamp from when the second tower fell. That's how I know.

RUTH FREMSON | Staff Photographer
The New York Times

NEW YORK: When I went outside, a cop said, "Don't go too far. The other one could go down any time." By the time I cleaned off my camera, cleaned off myself and called the desk, it was maybe two minutes before that rumbling started again. I ran back into the deli, and we ran into the stairwell that went into the basement. There couldn't have been more than 10 or 13 of us in there. Nobody knew what was happening. There was so much misinformation. We were hearing, "The White House has been hit. The Capitol had been hit. Chicago has been hit. Philadelphia was hit."

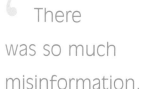

' There was so much misinformation. '

New York Times photographer Ruth Fremson (right), caught in the rubble while covering the first tower's collapse, walks with a Metropolitan Transit Authority police officer (center) as they and another man try to escape the dust cloud.

Tricia Meadows/Globe Photos

10:33

You couldn't see anything outside; it seemed like Armageddon. The only light was the bologna case glowing. Then smoke started coming up from the basement behind us. We didn't know if the building was stable. It smelled like something was on fire in the basement. One of the cops radioed a supervisor and said he was trapped in a deli with 10 people and needed to be evacuated.

At that point, one of the other firemen didn't think it was safe to wait in there. They started picking up rags on the deli counter, and everybody tied them around their faces. We went out holding hands. As we emerged from this cloud, I'm holding the hand of a Metropolitan Transit Authority police officer. She's the black woman whose hand I'm holding in the picture. I never saw the person take the picture. I didn't know about it until it appeared in *People.* I know it's me because I knew what I was wearing, and that was my bottle of looted water in my hand.

Then I was on the east side of the towers, the wind was blowing east, so all the smoke was blowing in my direction. You could hear secondary explosions, hear cars exploding. I knew we had other photographers at the site, so I started walking uptown. I saw one car coming and flagged him down — a man taking his wife, a trauma-care nurse, to Bellevue Hospital. I hitched another ride from a delivery truck. These guys were wonderful, packing in as many people as they could take.

‘ You couldn't see anything outside; it seemed like Armageddon. ’

TRICIA MEADOWS | Photographer
Globe Photos

NEW YORK: I was walking down Park Row taking pictures of people. Someone came over and handed me a rag, watered down with coffee. There weren't a lot of people where I was. I took one shot of a female photographer helping two transit workers across the street. I didn't see many other photographers down there. I only saw them on my way out, as they were trying to get into the area.

10:35

CAROL MARIN | Contributor
CBS News

NEW YORK: I told a fireman I worked for CBS News, and he said to walk in the middle of the street because there's debris falling. As he walks toward the tower, he turns and yells, "Run!" I hear simultaneously this roar and see what appears to be a gigantic fireball rising up at ground level. You could hear the tower begin to fall.

I turned and ran, and fell. A fireman grabbed me by the waist and threw me back on my feet, and we ran as fast as we could. He told me to take off my shoes, so I ran in my bare feet. Somewhere, the fireman threw me up against a wall and covered me with his body. All you really have at a moment like that is this giant sensory overload. It's what you smell, feel and hear, not what you geographically see in a large picture.

My face felt like it was pressed against cold marble. I felt him cover me, and I could feel the pounding of his heart against my backbone. The fireball hadn't reached us, but simultaneous with that recognition was a complete blackness. The air was filled with the particles of that falling building in a fierce, swirling cloud. There were things in the air — it was ash, it was granules, it was the atomized parts of desks and sinks and people, I realized later.

Somewhere along the line the fireman handed me off to a New York police officer, who was leading me through all this. I remember thinking that the fire and explosion didn't get us but the smoke will if we don't get out of it soon. He told me to cover my face, and I covered my mouth with my hand. It's all I had. Slowly, trying not to breathe, we kept pointing ourselves in the direction we believed was out of the cloud. Eventually the cloud lightened, and you could begin to see lightness. Suddenly we're out of the cloud. You're just out.

> The fireman threw me up against a wall and covered me with his body.

A man taking photographs turns and runs as the North Tower of the World Trade Center collapses.

JOHN BUSSEY | Foreign Editor
The Wall Street Journal

NEW YORK: There was a fireman standing next to me, and he said, "It's coming down! Run!" For a second, your mind clears and you think to yourself, "Run where?" What do you do when 110 stories collapse a couple of blocks away? So I ran after the fireman thinking that he would know where to run, and we dodged behind a wall.

A couple of other people ran with us. We were pressed against the wall of this building, where it all began to rain down on us. We could feel it on our backs and our shirts. Then, again, the lights went out — complete darkness. As you're crouching there, you are thinking many things. How long is this going to last? Are we going to survive? Are we, just one after the other, going to pass out from not getting enough oxygen?

The fireman we were with had a radio, and he was also a good coach. He was telling people to breathe in through your nose and not your mouth. He contacted over this radio another fireman, who was out with a respirator and a flashlight, and he found us crouching against the wall. It was like something out of a disaster movie. We put our hands on each other's shoulders, and then the fireman with the respirator led us just 20 steps, very close by but we didn't know it, into the lobby of a building.

> I wasn't a reporter anymore. I was just a refugee.

ROBERT J. HUGHES | Reporter
The Wall Street Journal

NEW YORK: The second tower fell, and people started screaming and running. An enormous cloud came over us again. At that point, I didn't stop to think about interviewing anyone. I wasn't a reporter anymore. I was just a refugee.

The North Tower collapses, sending an enormous cloud of debris and ash billowing through the streets. Many thought they were being buried alive when the dust covered them.

CATHERINE FITZPATRICK | Fashion Writer
Milwaukee Journal Sentinel

NEW YORK: I needed a phone. I had a dozen more interviews, and I needed to get them to the office. There was a guy and his wife opening a door to a warehouse. "Can I use a phone?" He's 55, round as a marble. He unlocked the door. Inside were two full-grown German shepherd guard dogs. Between the smoke smell and wailing sirens, the dogs were bashing themselves against an inner door. All I saw was dripping saliva and teeth. The warehouse owner says what every dog owner says, "They won't hurt you." He and his wife led me to the office, where I began to push buttons on his console phone. Finally I got connected to the newsroom and started dictating. The warehouse owner came in with this frosty cold bottle of Evian. I was so grateful I wept. But one of those dogs bit me on the ankle as soon as the guy walked out.

I left and headed south. I gotta get closer. Then it was black for me. That's when the building came down. I remember the ash cloud coming at me like Mount St. Helens, 40 stories high. Here's what I thought at the moment when I have every reason to expect to die. How many blocks away am I? How many stories high? How many feet long is a block? How many feet in a story? I can't do this math. I'm going to die in this ash cloud because I can't do the math.

> ' I'm going to die in this ash cloud because I can't do the math. '

Ernesto Mora/The Associated Press

Jeff Christensen/Reuters

In these two views of the North Tower collapse, it is evident that the building imploded, creating a mushroom cloud of debris.

CATHERINE LEUTHOLD | Photographer
Free-lance

NEW YORK: I could hear the building rumbling and it's the same sound. I knew this building was going to go. I remember what a war photographer had told me, and it popped into my head, "Make sure you always have an escape." The stores were all closed. I saw this subway hatch, and people coming out. I yelled, "Go back down. The North Tower is coming down." Someone swore at me. They wanted out of there. I wanted to go down there. All of a sudden it's happening again. I'm running. Everyone is running.

I decide I'm going to take pictures of the building coming down. I can barely stand it. "Hold on. Hold on." I'm gritting my teeth. I just want to get it. Then again, that whoosh. It pushed me into a revolving door. I ran into the elevator bank to escape the burning, and the smoke and the dust. Then I think, "No, this isn't a good place to be." Then we are in a circle with all these people, praying. We are holding each other really tight. Maybe 10 people. It was dark. It was smoky. Then I realize I have to start working again. I detach myself.

> ' I realize I have to start working again. ,

Free-lance photographer Catherine Leuthold documents her own and others' escape from the collapse of the North Tower.

Catherine Leuthold

GULNARA SAMOILOVA | Photo Retouch Artist
The Associated Press

NEW YORK: The AP doesn't have a black-and-white darkroom, so since I shot black and white, I had to go home to develop it. I have a darkroom in my kitchen. I walked home and mixed the chemicals. It's hot, and I put ice in to cool it off. As I was watching TV, I saw the second building start to collapse. I could hear it in my apartment. My building just jumped!

HAROLD DOW | Correspondent
"48 Hours," CBS News

NEW YORK: All of a sudden, I hear this freight train again. I think, "Oh shit, the second one is coming." I see this big plume of smoke from the second tower chasing me. You can't outrun these things. It engulfed me.

ARIS ECONOMOPOULOS | Staff Photographer
The Star-Ledger, Newark, N.J.

NEW YORK: I was standing 50 to 100 yards from the North Tower when I heard this metallic groaning sound. I looked up and saw the top of the North Tower teetering, while pieces of it fell toward me. I ran the fastest I ever ran in my life. While I'm running, I see this guy taking a picture of me. I'm thinking, "Are you crazy?" It was free-lance photographer Joe Tabacca.

Something hit my head — I think it was some aluminum siding. This startled me and almost knocked me off my feet. I was dazed, but I saw a big tour bus and quickly dove under the tires of the bus, along with Joe. Darkness descended on us, but I had already been through one of these toxic cloud things. I wasn't scared. I just wanted to get the hell out of there. Joe and I were shouting at each other, knowing there was a building behind us. We felt our way out, holding hands. We had to climb over a five-foot slab of concrete that had landed near us. That bus was a shield that saved our lives.

> " I ran the fastest I ever ran in my life. "

Star-Ledger photographer Aris Economopoulos flees the collapse of the North Tower, which he had been photographing.

10:42

Joe Tabacca

RICHARD DREW | Photographer
The Associated Press

> I held my
> finger on the
> trigger.

NEW YORK: I tried to hide myself in some high bushes in the median strip. I changed lenses to make some last pictures. While I was looking at the North Tower, it just poofed out like a mushroom. I held my finger on the trigger. It will shoot nine frames, so I held it down and made nine frames of the building coming down. I started running when the dust cloud came toward me.

I ran a block and a half to Stuyvesant High School. The lobby was filled with evacuated kids. I looked at the preview screen on my digital camera. This kid looking over my shoulder said, "Wow! What's that?"

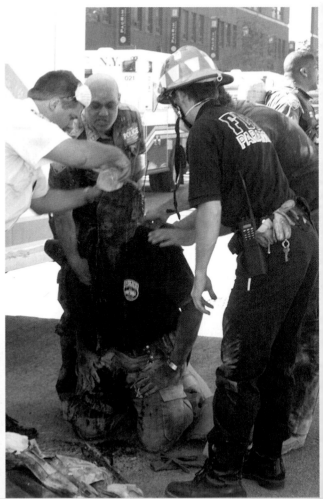

Photos by Richard Drew/The Associated Press

10:43

We went outside and I went south again, taking more pictures of debris and people. I couldn't see — it felt like there was silica in my eyes — so I went back into the high school to wash my face. Suddenly, the door slammed open and a cop yelled, "Everybody out! There's a gas leak in the basement!"

I made pictures of rescue workers on West Street. I remember the sound of all these Scott Air-Paks beeping as they ran out of air. A fireman shoved his face mask on me. There were no working phones. I tried to hire a messenger service van to take me back to the office. I had to walk back through the Village to Sixth Avenue to finally get a phone line to the office.

Far left: The North Tower collapse. Left: Rescue workers help an injured co-worker. Below: Pedestrians flee the area of the collapse.

10:44 A.M. CNN BREAKING NEWS — PENTAGON MONITORING SECOND SUSPECTED HIJACKED PLANE.

BOLÍVAR ARELLANO | Photographer
New York Post

NEW YORK: We heard the same sound as before, and everybody ran into the Financial Center. The explosion came down quickly and elevated us. I was elevated four feet into the air. I said to myself, "Bolivar, you screwed up. You survived the first one, but the second one is going to kill you." I crashed into the wall and then to the ground. I passed out for a few minutes. When I woke up, everything was dark. Two inches from my head was a piece of steel beam from the tower that had penetrated the building.

I went outside and heard voices saying, "Do you see the photographer? I'm sure he is dead." At that moment, I crossed the doorway and they were happy. I saw a lady on the ground who was bleeding, and I took a picture of her. Somebody brought a stretcher, and I took a picture of them carrying the lady out. My own leg was bloody and they tried to take me to the hospital but I said, "No, I can work."

> ' Do you see the photographer? I'm sure he is dead. '

Photographer Bolívar Arellano, caught in the collapse, documents rescue personnel evacuating an injured woman (below). Arellano also was injured — Matthew McDermontt captured this image (right) of Arellano's bloody leg.

Bolivar Arellano/New York Post

Matthew McDermontt/New York Post

DON HALASY | Photographer
New York Post

NEW YORK: The blast of air from the building coming down blew me up against a building. I started climbing up the wall but the weight of the debris was piled up on me. I stood up and made a little air pocket with my hands so I could breathe and lifted my hands over my head and started shoveling debris off my head. I must have been under seven or eight feet of debris. I finally got it down to shoulder level, and I was able to lift myself out. Later, a fireman came up to me and said, "You know something? You're bleeding." Both my arms and my left leg were cut open and blood was running down my arms and I didn't even realize it.

STAN HONDA | Photo Stringer
Agence France-Presse

NEW YORK: It made no sense at all. You couldn't figure out what was going on. Many people around me were extremely frightened and assuming the world was coming to an end, which at that point definitely seemed like it was happening.

MARIANNE McCUNE | Reporter
WNYC Radio

NEW YORK: I got my cell phone to work, and we called (WNYC local morning host) Mark Hilan, who was on the air. Beth Fertig and I were working as a team. I put Beth on the air in Foley Square. It was like my body reacted by trying to be a reporter, but my mind was trailing behind, saying this must be really serious. I called my family in California. My mother thanked me for calling. She said, "I know you have your job to do." Then she went into the back yard and cried.

We were still in that area when the second building collapsed. We were on the air with Mark, and you could hear us saying, "Oh my God, it's gone!"

> Oh my God, it's gone!

TODD MAISEL | Photographer
(New York) Daily News

> David is out in the middle of the floor. He's got no shelter at all.

NEW YORK: We made our way through the swirling dust into Battery Park City where we laid David Handschuh on the floor of a deli, its front door smashed. I gave him a Snapple and sat next to him for a brief moment before another rumble could be heard. Firefighters and cops dived back into the store, some screaming and crying. The second building sent debris hurtling toward our building, bringing down the façade and smashing windows.

After the second building came down, there was this incredibly terrifying moment when emergency rescuers were diving into the deli with us, screaming and yelling and crying. We were huddled together, but David was out in the middle of the floor. He's had no shelter at all.

That picture was like a 15th of a second, real slow. My flash was broken, and I didn't have much light. I hadn't cleaned my lens that well. But it really captured that terrifying moment. When the dust settled, a glimmer of light came through. It was like heaven's light.

New York *Daily News* photographer Todd Maisel captures his colleague David Handschuh, whose leg is broken, lying on the floor of a deli.

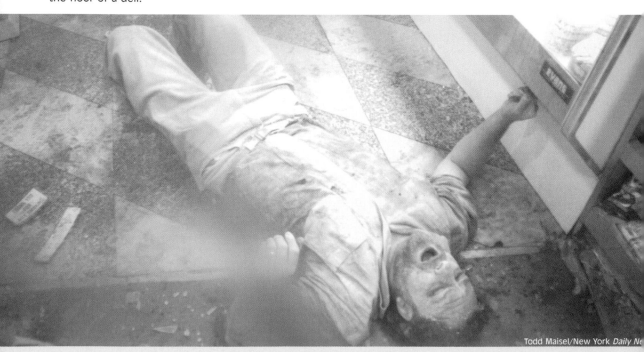

Todd Maisel/New York *Daily Ne*

GERALDINE BAUM | Reporter
Los Angeles Times

NEW YORK: I started walking after a man who looked like a businessman. As I interviewed him, we looked up and the second building fell. I'd just gotten his phone number. It looked to me that the tower and top had toppled over to the east. I thought, "Oh my God, what did it fall on?" We ran a little bit from the second building, but it was not as bad as the first one. After the second building fell, I decided it was time to unload my notes. The *Los Angeles Times* put out an extra edition. Kevin McNeal, whom I had just interviewed, was in the extra. I couldn't use my cell phone. I dialed the 800 number to the Washington bureau and said, "I'm here. Take a feed." Then I got out and started interviewing again. After the second (tower collapse), cops started pushing people back. I saw this 17-year-old take an empty bottle of water and fill it with dust. Already, the souvenir trade was beginning.

> ' I dialed the 800 number to the Washington bureau and said, `I'm here. Take a feed.' '

Suzanne Plunkett/The Associated Press

A man walks through the disaster area.

STEPHEN LUCAS | Director
"Today in New York," WNBC News

NEW YORK: Once the second tower got hit, everybody was focused on getting as many reporters to the field as possible. We were having sources come into the building. The entire city was in a lockdown. What a feeling of isolation it was, not to be able to leave or enter Manhattan. I've never witnessed anything like that before.

> He said, `I'm with the firemen and I'm safe and I'll meet you in 20 minutes.'

WENDY DOREMUS | Widow of
Photojournalist William Biggart

NEW YORK: I had my cell phone and Bill had his, but I could never reach him. After the first building went down, I called him and it finally went through. That was about 10:15 a.m., right after the first one went down. He said, "I'm with the firemen and I'm safe and I'll meet you in 20 minutes. I'm going over to West Street and I'll meet you there." He has a studio on West Street.

I got there and he wasn't there. I kept trying to call him on the cell, but just got his voice mail. I needed to get home to the kids so I left a note on the door, "Bill, I went home. Give me a call when you get here." I was still thinking he was caught up in the excitement of the whole thing.

Photographer William Biggart, who died in the collapse of the North Tower, captured these images on his last rolls of film. From left, workers evacuate an injured person, and firefighters set up a rescue effort.

Photos by William Biggart

www.quebecnewyo

ADAM LISBERG | Staff Writer
The Record, Hackensack, N.J.

NEW YORK: One of my editors came on the phone. I said, "Look, in case we get cut off, here's my wife and my mom's phone numbers. Tell them I'm OK." I figure I can feed my notes later. It was a very short conversation. Two firefighters came hopping through the window, and one said that the other building's going. I said, "Tim, I gotta go." All he heard was, "The other one's going." Click. I later heard that he said, "I think I may have just heard the last of Adam Lisberg."

> ' Here's my wife and my mom's phone numbers. Tell them I'm OK. ,

RICARDO ALVAREZ | News Director
Telemundo/Channel 47

TETERBORO, N.J.: The big problem was getting feeds. Our antenna was on top of the World Trade Center, and we went off the air when the second tower went down. We have direct feeds to all the cable systems, so we were not off the air completely. The phones were also a problem. We couldn't get through to our crews. We didn't know for a while where (reporter) Natalia (Cruz) was. We didn't know if she was gone or alive. She finally went to our live truck, and we knew she was OK.

William Biggart's final photos included a car covered in debris (left) and a firefighter walking from the site of the collapse as the traffic lights behind him continue to function.

0:50 A.M. **CNN — FIGHTER JETS SCRAMBLE AMID REPORTS OF SECOND PLANE HEADED FOR PENTAGON.**

JOHN DEL GIORNO | Helicopter Reporter
Metro Networks/
Shadow Broadcasting, WABC-?

NEW YORK: We continued up the West Side of Manhattan and actually got into a cluster with the other news helicopters at 79th Street. That was a matter of all the news helicopters working together. It was just extra eyes because you didn't know what was going to happen next. You had just seen the unbelievable happen. At 79th Street, I'm 13 blocks from the station, so they could communicate with me on a hand-held radio. The only word they received at that point was that more planes had been hijacked. We put the word out to the other news helicopters: keep your eyes open, we'll look to the left, you look to the right, and we'll stay here working together.

PAUL STEIGER | Managing Editor
The Wall Street Journal

NEW YORK: I'm in South Ferry Park trying to use my cell phone and can't get a line. I go to a pay phone, but of course the lines were all jammed. I thought, "If I ever get out of this, I'm always going to carry a roll of quarters with me." I got a dial tone. I assume if I had quarters, I could have made calls.

Then the second tower collapses. We're afraid we're going to get another tornado, but it's not so bad because the wind had shifted slightly.

There were all these wild rumors — some of them true — that the Pentagon and White House had been hit. I'm now kind of desperate. I want to find out about Wendy, my wife. I want to connect with our people to make sure nobody's been seriously hurt. I want to be sure we can put out a paper. But how do I get communications?

I decided the only thing to do was to get to my apartment, way up on the Upper East Side. Luckily, Rich Regis, a *Journal* deputy national editor, and I encountered buses that were part of an evacuation strategy. They were sent up the FDR Drive, up the East Side of Manhattan. So we climbed on the bus.

> If I ever get out of this, I'm always going to carry a roll of quarters with me.

PETER JENNINGS | Anchor and Senior Editor
ABC News

NEW YORK: The one imperative for anyone doing this job is absolute and total concentration, which is like protective clothing in some respects because you are so focused on what's happening that you don't have a lot of time for personal emotions. They come later.

My father was a great live broadcaster. He always told me when I was young, "If you are ever going to do this job, you have to pick your silences." I think a lot of people talk too much on television. I'm guilty of it, I'm sure. But what we call natural sound can be devastatingly powerful. When the buildings collapsed, that was a roar heard around the world. My inclination at times like this is to say as little as possible. Somebody wrote a piece later saying that when the towers collapsed, I put up my hands and told everybody to be quiet. Everybody who was near a television set or radio would be fully capable of interpreting this event for themselves. They didn't need me to do it for them. I have no hesitation with permitting silence on the air.

> **That was a roar heard around the world.**

The collapse of the second tower killed many rescue personnel.

Catherine Leuthold

10:52

JOAN ROSEN | New York State Photo Editor
The Associated Press

'Where's my father?'

NEW YORK: I got a call from (photographer) Dick Drew's daughter, who goes to school in Brooklyn. It was one of a lot of calls like that from family members. She said, "Where's my father?" I told her he was working, that he was OK, and I'd get back to her. But I didn't know if he was OK. We hadn't been able to reach him.

GULNARA SAMOILOVA, NEW YORK: I had three rolls to develop and then I saw there was one Ektachrome roll. Color slides! I was shocked. I don't know how it happened to be in my bag. AP needed color, so I developed the film. My girlfriend, who works at AP, called me. "Where have you been?" she asked. "I was *there*. I was photographing it," I said. She shouted out to the office, "Gulnara has film!" And they were like, "Come here as fast as you can."

I developed the film, washed it very fast and didn't even wait until it dried. I start walking toward the temporary office (that AP set up in midtown), shaking the negatives to dry. I got there and the scanner had problems, so I walked to the Rockefeller Center office. I took the slides to the lab and the editor said, "Gulnara, you've got some great stuff." I was one of the first photographers to arrive.

Gulnara Samoilova captured these images on the only roll of color film she had. From left: a man aids an injured woman who cannot walk; rescuers try to calm a woman who was badly burned.

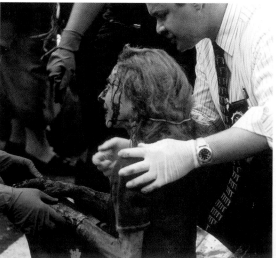

Photos by Gulnara Samoilova/The Associated Press

10:53 A.M. AP — NEW YORK'S PRIMARY ELECTIONS, SCHEDULED FOR TODAY, ARE POSTPONED.

YURI KIRILCHENKO | Senior Correspondent, New York Bureau
ITAR-TASS News Agency

NEW YORK: Some of it reminded me of scenes of World War II in Russia, when people gathered around radio transmitters to learn the latest news from the front. The similarity was quite striking. When I was wandering around the area of the catastrophe, I saw transmitters attached to the news tents and crowds of people gathered around them, everyone with intent expressions on their faces listening to the latest news. In this way, I was being updated every minute. You could pick up information at virtually every corner. Near Canal Street, people just carried their TV sets out to the street and crowds of people gathered around them.

> ' People just carried their TV sets out to the street and crowds of people gathered around them. '

Debris covers the streets near the area of the World Trade Center after the second collapse.

Gary Fabiano/*SIPA Press*

10:54 A.M. CNN — ISRAEL EVACUATES ALL DIPLOMATIC MISSIONS.

> I walked through the streets of Jersey City in a daze.

JIM PENSIERO | Assistant Managing Editor
The Wall Street Journal

JERSEY CITY, N.J.: I walked through the streets of Jersey City in a daze. Fighter planes were overhead. You heard people listening to their radios in the car, and you knew now the Pentagon had been attacked. I was thinking, "OK, this is a real major attack."

The PATH (train) station was closed, but I kept walking west to the other PATH station, which was open. I got a PATH out to where my car was parked. I tried at that point to call my wife but couldn't get through. Eventually I got my car phone to work. Her first words to me were — this will probably get censored but, you know, she was upset that I hadn't called — "You asshole." "Ha!" I said, "I'm alive." She was relieved. I knew she was OK, and I knew the kids were OK.

The smoke from the World Trade Center towers could be seen clearly from Jersey City, N.J.

Daniel Hulshizer/The Associated Press

10:55

Mark Lennihan/The Associated Press

GERALD M. BOYD | **Managing Editor**
The New York Times

Pedestrians flee across the Brooklyn Bridge. Roads and tunnels were closed, leaving many people no choice but to walk.

NEW YORK: You really would have to have been here to understand what that day was like. Subways were being stopped. There were bomb threats all over the place. Buildings were being evacuated. It was an incredibly confusing time, and no one knew what was going on. So we had that dynamic, which was potentially a dynamic of uncertainty on the part of all of us. Not fear, but uncertainty, coupled with a dynamic of staff members who had actually been there or lived in Lower Manhattan and had seen firsthand the aftermath of what happened. They had a whole different set of emotions. We had a graphics editor who was down there sketching. If she had run one way, she dies. She ended up fleeing with everyone else across the Brooklyn Bridge.

We were basically on automatic pilot because we had a job to do. But we had other people in the *Times* family who don't work in the newsroom who were experiencing this. There were people throughout the building walking up to the metro desk or calling me, asking what they could do.

> We were basically on automatic pilot because we had a job to do.

RICHARD PYLE | Reporter
The Associated Press

> ❛ These people were scared, dazed, angry, some crying. ❜

NEW YORK: We headed across the Brooklyn Bridge. We were like salmon swimming upstream against the flood of people coming the other way from Manhattan. These people were scared, dazed, angry, some crying, many covered with ash that made it look as if they'd aged 30 years in five minutes. Maybe some of them had. I interviewed people on the bridge, including one who had seen the wing of the plane go by his office window.

The South Tower had collapsed while I was on the train, and we were halfway across the bridge when the North Tower suddenly went down right before our eyes, with an indescribable rumble-screech and a huge billowing of dust. The people fleeing Manhattan looked back in horror. There was a large collective groan of agony. Some screamed; some panicked and tried to run through the crowd ahead.

People flee on foot across the Brooklyn Bridge.

Daniel Shanken/The Associated Press

10:57 A.M. CNN — **N.Y. GOV. GEORGE PATAKI SAYS ALL STATE GOVERNMENT OFFICES ARE CLOSED.**

HERNANDO REYES SMIEKER | Reporter
Noticias 1380

NEW YORK: I see thousands and thousands of people walking across the bridge. Then I see Pauline (Liu) from Channel 11 (WPIX-TV), the only familiar face I recognize. I start to cry. Maybe that's the reaction when you see a familiar face. I start to cry like a baby and couldn't stop. I'm sorry, I'm a reporter, I'm not supposed to cry, but I'm shaking, I feel so bad.

Daniel Shanken/The Associated Press

> ' I'm sorry. I'm a reporter. I'm not supposed to cry. '

The exodus from New York City was chaotic, with people pushing to get to the head of the crowd and some stopping to look back in disbelief.

10:58

11:18

11:19 A.M. AP Bulletin: New York — In Pa., a large plane believed to be a 747 crashed.

CNN LIVE — BREAKING NEWS

Aaron Brown: "*We have reports that a plane has crashed in the Pittsburgh area southeast of Pittsburgh about 80 miles. And at varying times we have heard this was a 767 or a 747; I'm not sure it matters which it is. What matters is that a plane has crashed in the Pittsburgh area.*"

SCOTT SPANGLER | **Photographer**
Tribune-Review, Greensburg, Pa.

GREENSBURG, Pa.: The FAA (Federal Aviation Administration) had said to land all the planes. I raced to the airport terminal, thinking I'd be shooting people coming out of the local terminal. I raced into the terminal and went right into a meeting in the airport management offices. You work in a small town, you know everybody. They let me right in. I met with Dwayne Pickels, our reporter. At this time, they knew United Flight 93 is hijacked and in our airspace.

They were listening to the control tower. There was a man in the tower who could see the plane. The flight line was 12 miles from the tower. Airport security officials were listening to the tower guy. They wanted to shut down the airport and get people out. At the airport, there were probably 100 people. I remember distinctly standing next to Dwayne, and a guy came in and was listening to one of the walkie-talkies. He looked right at us, and said, "It's down. It crashed."

I ran through the airport, through the parking lot to my car. I usually carry a full bag of lenses and two camera bodies. Average weight on your shoulder is a good 50 pounds. Dwayne

> He looked right at us, and said, "It's down. It crashed."

just stayed. I knew exactly where it was. My family has a campground near that area. I knew the backwoods. I did not wait for anybody.

I've got a scanner in the car, and they were calling for every police officer. They were broadcasting they had a plane down. I could hear a fire crew saying there was heavy smoke. Because they said it was hijacked, I knew it had to be related. My heart was pounding. I was sweating. I emotionally was a wreck. I knew from prior experience of the past USAir crash that it was not going to be pretty.

I was driving really fast, still looking for smoke. I knew my dad was en route to Chicago. I made the fatal mistake of calling my mother. She was watching TV. She couldn't get a hold of my father or me or my brother. As soon as she heard my voice, she screamed, "Please don't go, Scotty! Get the hell out of there! I can't go through this!" I just had to hang up.

> " Please don't go, Scotty! Get the hell out of there! "

RICK EARLE | Westmoreland Co. Bureau Chief
WPXI-TV

GREENSBURG, Pa.: My photographer and I were packing and getting ready to leave to drive to New York. I ran to the grocery store to pick up some bottled water and chips, snacks, crackers. I was in the grocery store in the checkout line, and a guy came in. He said, "My brother said there's just been a plane crash in Acme." His brother worked at the airport.

I ran out to my car, called 911 to the emergency dispatcher. I'm the Westmoreland County bureau chief for WPXI. I've been here seven years. I talk to emergency dispatchers several times a day normally. They said, "We don't have anything confirmed, just reports of a plane down." I called my station, alerted them and said, "I'm checking this out."

I called the emergency dispatcher back. They had finally nailed it down. I called the station back while waiting for the photographer and gave the exact location. At that point, they said, "Go check that out. Forget about New York."

11:23 A.M. AP NEWSALERT — AMERICAN AIRLINES SAYS IT "LOST" TWO OF ITS AIRCRAFT.

KEITH SRAKOCIC | Staff Photographer
The Associated Press

PITTSBURGH: We heard they'd shut down all the airports. A reporter and I jumped in the car and headed for Pittsburgh International. We got out there, and they wouldn't let us near the terminal. I was shooting what I could. Then I got a phone call from my editor in Philadelphia who told us that a plane had crashed in Shanksville (Pa.). I didn't know where it was. I had to leave the reporter at the airport, and he had to get back on his own.

I jumped into my car and headed out. As I drove, I listened to the radio and had time to think. The feeling was of personal loss. I had covered a USAir crash earlier, where it was a more typical news gathering. There, you didn't feel as though it was something happening to you. But this crash did not feel that way. It felt personal.

I thought there would be a pseudo-media command center, remembering how little access there was in the first plane crash and was amazed at how much better the attitude was.

RACHEL R. SNYDER | Staff Reporter
Daily Courier, Connellsville, Pa.

CONNELLSVILLE, Pa.: We didn't know exactly where to go. We knew how to get to Shanksville (Pa.), but it was maybe an hour's drive. Somerset is one of our neighboring counties. We don't usually cover anything that far, but this was a big story. We didn't know if it had anything to do with the terrorist attack at that time.

We found it because we saw other TV trucks and we followed them. I was scared when I first found out that I had to go. I didn't know if something more was going to happen. If there were terrorists on the plane, what if they were still alive? What else could happen? I didn't say, "No, I won't go." When you're a newspaper reporter and something like this happens, you're scared but it's an opportunity.

> When you're a newspaper reporter and something like this happens, you're scared, but it's an opportunity.

JON MEYER | Reporter
WJAC-TV

JOHNSTOWN, Pa.: A photographer and I ran out (and got) into the live truck and headed in that direction. Within about 25 minutes we were near that area. I had a portable scanner in the car. That gave us a chance to hear them give emergency crews directions. Eventually we caught up with some of the firetrucks and ambulances heading into the scene. That helped us get right to the road near the actual crash site.

I got out of the car, ran up over the hill and ran down where the crater was. We were so early that they hadn't had a chance to set up a barrier for the press. I ran ahead of the cameraman while he went to get his camera. I was able to get right up to the edge of the crater. The photographer was less than a minute right behind me, but they stopped him because they saw his camera. No one else got beyond that barrier.

There was just a big hole in the ground. All I saw was a crater filled with small, charred plane parts. Nothing that would even tell you that it was the plane. I could tell something very large had crashed, and the smell of jet fuel was strong. You just can't believe a whole plane went into this crater. First thought I had was, "I've gotta write down what I'm seeing." I could see some charred trees and smoke off in the woods. It was only a matter of minutes before police said, "You've got to get out." There were no suitcases, no recognizable plane parts, no body parts. The crater was about 30 to 35 feet deep.

I ran around trying to ask different rescue crews if they could tell me anything. I felt we needed to tell people what's going on here. No emergency crews would tell me anything. We did get a couple of eyewitnesses who lived around there and saw the plane come really low or heard the crash and came to see what had happened. When I couldn't find any officials, I went back to our live truck, got on the phone and told the anchor over the air what I'd seen.

> All I saw was a crater filled with small, charred plane parts.

Scott Spangler/Tribune-Review

Journalists were kept about a mile from the Pennsylvania crash site. Only a handful who arrived before rescue workers actually saw the site.

SCOTT SPANGLER, SHANKSVILLE, Pa.: I saw the smoke. It was in this reclaimed stripmine area. Everything was barren and stripped except for this funky, weedy dried grass. I pulled over, jumped out, popped the trunk, grabbed every camera I had and started running.

My cell phone was ringing. My brother screamed at the top of his lungs, "Don't go there!" I had the earpiece on. I'm running down the field toward the crash site. "It's my job. I've gotta go," I said and hung up because I needed my hands free.

I was running with this 50-pound bag, a cell phone in my left hand, a camera body with a long lens in my right hand. The terrain was rugged. I was trying to watch my step, run and shoot at the same time. I didn't think I was in the right place. I was looking for a wing or a tail. There was nothing, just this pit. I panned with my cameras for a panorama, trying to take a tight picture across this 400-yard area. I was looking for anything that said tail, wing, plane, metal. There was nothing.

> ❝ I'm looking for a wing or a tail. There's nothing, just this pit. ❞

RICK EARLE, En route to SHANKSVILLE, Pa.: We headed there. I was working the phones. I called the 911 dispatcher to check with him about 10 or 15 minutes later to see what the latest was. He said, "You are not going to believe this. We got a call from a guy who claimed to be a passenger on the plane." I was taking it all down as we were driving along. I said, "What did he say?" The dispatcher said that he gave the right plane model. And he said that it was an emergency, that a plane had been hijacked.

> Earle phoned his station and broke this story on the air:
>
> "I just a few minutes ago talked again to the Westmoreland County Public Safety Department. He does tell me that it is apparently a United Airlines jet. He says it has crashed in Shanksville. I asked him how they found out about this. Amazingly, he said at 9:58 a.m. this morning his 911 center received a cell phone call from a person claiming to be a passenger onboard that United flight. He said the passenger told him that the plane was now being hijacked. He (the passenger) said repeatedly, 'This is not a hoax. This is not a hoax. This is not a hoax.'
>
> "He said that he was at this point being walked back to the bathroom of the plane. (The) 911 (operator) was talking to him trying to get more information at that time. The gentleman who had made the call from the airplane said there was just an explosion, then there was a cloud of white smoke, and then seconds later they lost the caller."

'This is not a hoax.

This is not a hoax.

This is not a hoax.'

We kept driving, got to the scene about the same time as a local NBC affiliate from Johnstown. We own the station in Johnstown. They were a big help. They were in the process of establishing a live shot when we pulled up, having gotten a couple of interviews already.

After we reported the phone call, the 911 center was deluged with phone calls. A lot of people didn't know the plane crash was related to terrorists. But as the day went on, everything the caller said turned out to be true. At the time, the dispatcher is telling me about the call, we were skeptical. We did not give the flight number because we did not want to scare people, and we didn't have any confirmation. All we had is a phone call from a guy who said he was on the plane.

JON MEYER, SHANKSVILLE, Pa.: We were able to get our live truck established, set up the signal and have the crash scene in the background. Because we had a microwave truck and could establish a signal, and because we were there so quickly, we were able to do reports before anyone.

Then the local police came and said, "You have to move or you'll be arrested." So we got permission from the strip mine operator since the plane crashed in an old strip mine, to establish a signal elsewhere on his property. So you could still see it (the crash site) in the background.

Then we started doing reports from there. At this point, we had two reporters. Another reporter I work with from Channel 6 (WJAC-TV) came after about 20 minutes. Then the state police surrounded us and told us we had to move. Then they set up a media staging area and we had to go to that, and you couldn't even see the crash (site). After that, the FBI tightly controlled any access to the site.

> We were able to do reports before anyone.

RACHEL R. SNYDER, CONNELLSVILLE, Pa.: When we got there, they were not allowing media to go to the crash site. There were media trucks parked at the edge of the cornfield. They were lined up and down the road, at least 50 different stations, radio, newspapers, TV. I was in awe because I made acquaintances with people from *The New York Times*, *Sunday Times* in London, CNN. It was a chance of a lifetime. I'm only 25, so that was a big experience for me.

KEITH SRAKOCIC, SHANKSVILLE, Pa.: I got there relatively late. Drive time was about an hour. There were already satellite trucks and massive amounts of media assembled. I was amazed. There seemed to be a much less hostile attitude toward the media there. I felt like we were seen as doing a service. We were getting information to the people who needed it, as opposed to the common perception of intruding. There was more respect for what we did.

I drove into this side-road farm field. One of our freelancers was there, Gary Trematina. We were taking turns looking at what we could shoot. We couldn't see the crash scene at all. Gary and I drove into suburban Shanksville, stopped and asked people to use their telephone line to transmit pictures. They were very accommodating and very helpful.

I figured it would be days to see the crash site, but they actually did take bus tours in there that day. I'd say we were a half mile away from the hole.

STEPHEN LUCAS | Director
"Today in New York," WNBC News

NEW YORK: Our general manager, Dennis Swanson, came into the control room and said, "They are evacuating 30 Rock (Rockefeller Center). Everybody should leave the building. If you want to stay, it's strictly voluntary." Nobody from the crew got up. This was our job. We are journalists, and we've got to get the story out, even if the building was going to go down. We stayed and we covered the story.

JOAN ROSEN | New York State Photo Editor
The Associated Press

NEW YORK: Our PA (public address) system started saying, "Leave the building. Leave the building." I'm thinking, "Oh God, what next? Will Rockefeller Center be next?"

> ' We've got to get the story out, even if the building was going to go down. '

KILEY ARMSTRONG | Assignment Editor, New York Bureau
The Associated Press

NEW YORK: Somewhere around 11 a.m. they ordered our building evacuated, but we didn't go.

MARCUS BRAUCHLI | National News Editor
The Wall Street Journal

NEW YORK: I have a DSL (digital subscriber line) in my apartment. Though I could get few phone calls out, I was able to marshal coverage. I sent hundreds of e-mails in the next few hours. The first was a note telling all bureaus that we would have a paper.

> All bureaus: (10:52 a.m.)
> We're obviously not in the office. We'll be relocating our editing operation to New Jersey, to our backup site. Phone lines in the northeast are jammed, and so you may not be able to reach us. For the time being, please start calling your companies to find out if any of their top people are missing in the catastrophes. You should also call local and federal officials in your area, to know of any threats or actions they are aware of, or any moves they are making.
> Many thanks and best,
> Brauchli, New York

JOANNE LIPMAN | Weekend Journal Editor
The Wall Street Journal

NEW YORK: Since no one could reach anybody on the phones, all day long, on e-mail, on BlackBerry (wireless hand-held e-mail), you would get these messages. No one knew who was where. So every message was sent to the whole staff. You would see hundreds of messages that were one line — a subject line, reporter's name, and it would say, "Have my laptop, I'm ready to work."

> You would see ... messages ... that would say, 'Have my laptop, I'm ready to work.'

Aris Economopoulos/The Star-Ledger, Newark, N.J.

Photographer Aris Economopoulos took this shot of firefighters working in the rubble of the World Trade Center below an eerie sky.

ARIS ECONOMOPOULOS | Staff Photographer
The Star-Ledger,
Newark, N.J.

> You want to shoot with tact, but this is a news story.

NEW YORK: I was shooting everything. You want to shoot with tact, and respect your subject matter, but this is a news story. Everybody, including myself, was part of the story. There was this eerie, dark black smoke with this orange glow coming through the sun. Some of my pictures, it's just amazing to see them.

(*New York Post* photographer) Don (Halasy) thought I was underneath the rubble. He didn't know where I went after the second tower collapsed. He got hold of his desk and his desk contacted my desk. My desk thought I was underneath the rubble for about three hours. There were at least one or two other photographers they hadn't heard from.

BETH FERTIG | Reporter
WNYC Radio

NEW YORK: We walked around and saw people taken to a makeshift triage center in the entrance of the city health department. It was the strangest scene in the lobby. There was a man with a broken arm, taped up with a ruler and masking tape. There were all these doctors wearing West Nile virus T-shirts trying to help people who were fleeing this catastrophe. The only emergency they were prepared for was West Nile virus.

We found a woman who worked on the 82nd floor (of one tower) who had seen people fleeing with their skin burned off. It was hard to get people to talk because they were so distraught. Many only agreed to talk so their families would hear them and know they were safe.

> There was a man with a broken arm, taped up with a ruler and masking tape.

CAROL MARIN | Contributor
CBS News

NEW YORK: I saw a CBS satellite truck and a WCBS cameraman who'd been hit make his way out of the truck, his forehead all bloody. Folks at the truck said, "Come on the air." I was on briefly from that location in a live shot to local news. They were local reporters. They were very nice. They made me sit down. I tried to blot the blood on his forehead.

RICHARD PYLE | Reporter
The Associated Press

NEW YORK: I went uptown on foot, talking to people along the way. I talked to people who had seen the plane, seen it hit, escaped the collapse. At every pay phone, there were 10 to 12 people in line. I finally got a phone and dictated a story about the evacuation of Lower Manhattan.

LINGLING SUN | General Manager
China Daily Distribution Corp.

> ' I had to tell my people that I was OK. '

NEW YORK: I had to tell my people that I was OK. We have a printing shop in Brooklyn, but at that moment, all the phone numbers in my head disappeared. All I could remember was my husband's phone number in Jamaica. I couldn't call it because it was long distance. I had a business card from a gift shop in Manhattan. I used my only quarter, wished myself good luck, and someone answered. I told them, "I'm just out of the World Trade Center, and I have to make a phone call but I don't have any money." They said, "Don't talk about money! Give us your husband's phone number."

TOM FLYNN | Producer
CBS News

NEW YORK: I rode my bike north along with all these people who were streaming up, some looking like I did. I was covered with dust. At 23rd Street, where the Chelsea Piers are, they handed me a cup of water. It was heaven-sent. My eyes and throat were killing me. I got back on the bike. Put the cup back in my bag. I still have it.

I got here to work and got stopped by a guard who demanded to see my ID. I was pretty wobbly and showed him my ID. When I got into the newsroom a lot of people were worried about me. I knew about the second one (tower) falling because when it went down, I saw it on the people's faces. I heard a chorus of, "Oh, no!"

When I got into the office, Dan (Rather) was on the air. They asked me, "Would you tell him what you saw?" I was on the air at 10:55 a.m. with Dan.

Eddie Remy (whom Flynn deputized to shoot for CBS) had gotten on one of those boats to New Jersey. We had a truck feeding from Liberty State Park but he wasn't able to get in there. Unfortunately, he was shooting the North Tower when the South went.

GERALDINE BAUM | Reporter
Los Angeles Times

NEW YORK: I saw a little second-hand bookshop. This old lady was letting people in, one at a time, to use the phone. She let me in, and I sat in a chair. I still hadn't called my husband. I was incredibly worried about my children. My nanny was going to come in on the train from Long Island. I was obsessed with it. My kids were in school until 3 p.m. I called my husband several times and couldn't get him. I finally got his secretary and said, "I cannot go on with my day until I know that my kids will be picked up from school." I was very agitated. It worked out. The nanny somehow got in at 9 a.m. She went to the school and picked my kids up.

MARCY McGINNIS | Senior Vice President, News Coverage
CBS News

NEW YORK: The very first day is the only day that we agreed to share what video we had with all the other networks. Because we were in the middle of what we really thought was a national crisis, CBS thought it would be a good idea to talk to our counterparts.

(CBS News President) Andrew (Heyward) called CNN, ABC and NBC. He talked to the presidents of those (news) divisions, and they all agreed. So for the first day, we declared what's ours is yours, and what's yours is ours.

On the second day we went back to business as usual. It was a deal we made until the end of that first day. It's kind of an unprecedented thing for us to do but so was this event. The phone call went to other networks between 11 a.m. and noon, I'm going to guess.

Tons of people came in or called with video. Some called and said I have something for you. Some walked in with video. Some went to a transmission truck near the site. Some people were asking for money, some for a lot, some for a little.

> The very first day is the only day we agreed to share what video we had with all the other networks.

JOAN ROSEN, NEW YORK: All of a sudden, an endless stream of people with photographs started coming in — students, workers, people who had a camera and were there. We put through all the film and looked at everything. Some were junk. Some were great! We negotiated a price. Some asked for a lot of money, and I had to phone our executive photo editor. The earlier you got here, the better. At the beginning we paid a lot because we didn't know what we had (from AP reporters in the field). The average was between $500 and $2,000.

> An endless stream of people with photographs started coming in.

There was a young man who worked for a guy from Hong Kong who had done work for AP. His name was Chao Soi Cheong. He had photos of the burning towers, including the dramatic moment of impact when the second hijacked plane hit. I asked, "How much do you want?" He said, "I just want my name used." I had to insist that he take some money. We agreed on $300. I wrote on his bill, "Increase." I paid him considerably more afterward. The next day one of his photographs ran full page on the front page of *USA TODAY*. It also appeared on the cover of *U.S. News (& World Report)*.

Carmen Taylor, a tourist from Arkansas, actually photographed the second plane hitting the tower. She e-mailed it to a TV person in Arkansas. They were a member (of The Associated Press), so they called AP. We moved it and then pulled it back because no one could confirm it (was not a hoax). It took us all day to confirm. It wasn't until 10 that night that we were able to send a photographer to her hotel to talk to her and transmit it.

We had a dentist who photographed the plane going into the tower from Brooklyn. We sent a photographer in Brooklyn to look at it in his office. *Newsweek* eventually bought it.

BARBARA WOIKE | Photo Editor, NYC Bureau
The Associated Press

NEW YORK: I burned up an incredible amount of time on the dentist (who was offering photos for sale). I sent a photographer to his office to look at the pictures. He wanted to sell them to me without me seeing them. He was trying to start a bidding war. He used up a lot of precious time.

A photographer named Mark Phillips had sent us pictures of smoke coming out of the first tower. We got them out quickly on the wire. Later, we heard that there was a rumor that there was a devil's face in the smoke in his picture (which proved untrue).

KRISTEN BROCHMANN | Photographer
Free-lance

NEW YORK: My thinking was if there's anything on my film of the second plane and if it's going to be used for anything, it's gotta be quick. I figure I'm not the only one who photographed the second plane going in. I've never done any news photography.

I dropped the film (to be developed) and walked to 36th and Eighth Avenue to my friend's office. They didn't have a television there, but they had a high-speed Internet connection and we were watching live feeds from CNN and MSNBC. This was about 11 a.m. I walked back to the film lab. It cost about $6.50. Then I walked up to *The New York Times*. I walked to the receptionist and said, "I have some pictures of the second plane going into the building."

A young guy came down and took me up to the third floor. When I got there, it was pretty calm. One photographer had just come in with a scarf wrapped around his face for breathing purposes. There were a lot of photographers there. One guy was taking my name and Social Security number; another guy scanned (my photos). I must say the *Times* was very gracious. The executive editor came up and shook my hand, saying really sincerely, "Thanks for bringing these to the *Times*." Jim Wilson, the photo director, sat me down and said, "Here's the deal. If we use it on the inside we'll pay $500. If on the front, obviously it will be more." They didn't pay me because they never ran it. They did sell it to *Newsweek*.

> I figure I'm not the only one who photographed the second plane going in.

David Frank/The New York Times

New York Times Executive Editor Howell Raines (second from left) and Managing Editor Gerald M. Boyd (third from left) choose photographs for the newspaper's September 12 layout.

> That moment of seeing the photographs was journalistically freeing.

HOWELL RAINES | Executive Editor
The New York Times

NEW YORK: I remember being very concentrated on making sure we were doing the right big things. I kept asking myself, "What are the things we ought to be doing that we are not?" I was very concerned about the visuals. I went to see Jim Wilson and Margaret O'Connor in the photo department. I was introduced to a man, a free-lancer who had come in off the street. He had just brought in his images. I remember it specifically. I don't even want to use the word relax, but I did relax once I knew we were covered on the central image. "Thanks for thinking of us," I said, and shook his hand. That moment of seeing the photographs was journalistically freeing. I knew, early in the day, we had key images for the paper.

JIM PENSIERO | Assistant Managing Editor
The Wall Street Journal

SOUTH BRUNSWICK, N.J.: I got here at about 11:20 a.m. I think I was the first person to show up. When I got here, the rooms were already prepared. Jesse Lewis, the copy chief, was here, and his e-mail was working. (Managing editor) Paul (Steiger) wasn't here, and I was very worried about him. I saw the (tower) fall, and I thought anybody in or anybody near that, it wouldn't go well for them.

MARCUS BRAUCHLI, NEW YORK: Beside my computer, I kept two lists in pen on a pad of paper. One was a list of reporters and editors who had contacted me by e-mail and were available to work. Some I dispatched to report or to New Jersey to edit. Others I told to stand by.

The other list contained the names of people I knew of who were in the vicinity of the World Trade Center and who were missing.

Early on, I had received an e-mail from Peter Kann, Dow Jones' chairman and CEO, and international president Karen Elliott House, who were in Hong Kong, where it was nearly midnight. Unable to reach anyone by phone, they and I set up an e-mail exchange. I kept them posted on who was missing and who had been accounted for. At the top of our (missing) list: managing editor Paul Steiger. At one point, I sent an e-mail to all the remaining people.

> The list contained the names of people I knew were missing.

To: Steiger, Hertzberg, Pensiero, Panagoulias, Bussey
11:35 a.m.
Can each of you pls confirm receipt of this when you get it, copied to us all?
Many thanks,
Marcus

CATHY PANAGOULIAS | Assistant Managing Editor
The Wall Street Journal

NEW YORK: At one point I saw a message from Marcus (Brauchli) to the top editors saying, "Please acknowledge receipt of this message." It was copied to Phil Revzin, an editor in Hong Kong, and I knew that (chairman and CEO) Peter Kann was using Phil's machine.

I thought if Marcus copied this to Phil and to Peter, they must think somebody's dead. But I didn't know what they were thinking until hours later when I realized it was Steiger they were worried about.

> To: Revzin, Phil (11:38 a.m.)
> From: Brauchli, Marcus
> As you will surmise, haven't heard from any of them since WTC collapse. But Steiger ordered the move to SB, so he may be in transit.

WENDY DOREMUS | Widow of photographer William Biggart

NEW YORK: I walked home. I got my son, who was uptown, and found out that little Bill (Biggart's eldest son) was all right. We live near St. Vincent's Hospital. They had set up a crisis center where you could turn in the name of a missing person. Nobody really knew what to do. I went over there with little Bill. There's a feeling in the pit of your stomach that this just couldn't be happening. I was hoping that he was with the other photojournalists. I was thinking he had just gotten into the shoot.

Bill was somebody who always came home. He was a Cancer crab — he loved his home. He would call constantly. We talked 10 to 12 times a day, so I knew there was a problem if he hadn't called me. I kept coming up with reasons to think positively.

> There's a feeling in the pit of your stomach that this just couldn't be happening.

ARSHAD MOHAMMED | White House Correspondent
Reuters

ABOARD AIR FORCE ONE: At 11:20 (a.m.), Gordon Johndroe (White House aide in charge of the press pool) came to talk to us. He said the president is keeping abreast, and the vice president is safe. Then he talked to us off the record and told us we were going to Barksdale Air Force Base near Shreveport, Louisiana. "This is a national security emergency. The president is going to be evacuated." He told us we couldn't report it even as we got there. At some point, we were told to turn off our pagers and phones. Even when we landed on the ground, we couldn't call our desks.

Gordon said once the president made a statement that we could then report that the president reported this at an undisclosed location. I repeated this to him so he understood how bad this sounded. Did he really feel that the president should be quoted from an undisclosed location? Wouldn't that make the country feel more tense?

Another extraordinary thing was the airmen in full combat fatigues with automatic weapons who immediately surrounded this plane. They were putting combat personnel around his plane at an Air Force base that nobody knew he was flying to. That's an indication of how much concern there was for his safety. The guy in charge of these combat airmen yelled, "Hey, get to that wingtip. Now!" This showed their level of tension. Another thing was odd. Normally there's a very elaborate motorcade. The president travels in large limousines or bullet-proof SUVs. But he got into a nonstandard vehicle, unlike the armored limousines he normally rides in.

When we got to where Bush was going to give a statement, we still couldn't call our desks. Somebody told Gordon that the local TV channel was saying the president was at Barksdale. So Gordon said, "OK, you can call your desk." That was a good, quick, correct decision. "Fine, if it's out there, you can report it," he said. That's when I first called the desk with bulletins.

> This is a national security emergency. The president is going to be evacuated.

Win McNamee/Reuters

White House reporters traveling with President Bush ask questions during an impromptu press conference at Barksdale Air Force Base in Louisiana.

SONYA ROSS | White House Reporter
The Associated Press

> I ... scribbled notes with my left hand in really bad "Sonya-hand."

BARKSDALE AIR FORCE BASE, La.: Wheels were down at 11:45 a.m. We got off the plane, and there were guys in camouflage with M-16s, and very few people on the tarmac. We took a short five-vehicle motorcade away from the plane to a nearby building and waited under the shade of a tree while Bush made a brief phone call inside. Then we went to a conference room in a second building where Bush taped his televised statement. I called AP from my cell (phone). As I was on the phone, Bush entered and began making his statement. I held out the phone so my colleague could hear Bush. I had the phone and tape recorder in my right hand and scribbled notes with my left hand in really bad "Sonya-hand."

The White House press escort told us that they were narrowing the (press) pool from 12 to five journalists. At this point, I've gone beyond just reporting for the AP and have become the eyes and ears for magazines and newspapers, too. Everybody's duties get broader. Being the pool reporter is tough. I felt a huge responsibility not to hang on to information for glory's sake.

ARSHAD MOHAMMED, BARKSDALE AIR FORCE BASE, La.:

The president came and spoke to us. Afterward, he took no questions. We raced into a room next door. I grabbed the phone and started dictating. We were there about 20 minutes. Then they herded us into a bus and (White House press aide) Gordon (Johndroe) told us who was going to continue on with the (press) pool. My recollection was that he said they were shrinking everything, including the press. They took the AP photographer and correspondent, Ann Compton (ABC News), who was doing radio but is very experienced in TV, and the CBS TV crew.

We were standing on the tarmac, watching everyone else get on the plane. I didn't argue because there was no point. They made the stipulation that (AP reporter) Sonya (Ross) would file for all of us, acting as a pool reporter.

It was clear they were not going to change their minds on this. They said they were going to arrange a plane to fly us back to Washington. The plane was set up for White House officials and they took us, too. It's sort of amazing that they got us back to D.C. that same day when planes were locked down all over the country.

We had a couple more hours in Barksdale and I filed a color story. We got back on a plane and I was home by 6 or 7.

> They got us back to D.C. that same day when planes were locked down all over the country.

DEY ST

ONE ...Y

...I'll never tell.

MICHAEL DOUGLAS
DON'T SAY
A WORD
9-28-01

Cortland Street
Station

F.D.N.Y.

AMBULANCE

12:22

12:23 P.M. **AP** NewsAlert: New York — Police official says casualties could be in thousands.

2 planes destroy World Trade Center.

CBS NEWS

ATTACK ON AMERICA

Dan Rather: *"Dateline: New York. A police official speaking on condition of anonymity says that the number of Trade Center casualties, still unknown, could be, quote, 'in the thousands.'"*

CATHERINE FITZPATRICK | Fashion Writer
Milwaukee Journal Sentinel

NEW YORK: Because the Verizon towers came down, my cell phone didn't work. To get a line back to the newsroom to phone in pieces of interviews for a timeline, I waved a $50 bill to people talking on their cell phones. Nobody took my money, and everybody gave me their phones.

SUSAN WATTS | Photographer
(New York) Daily News

NEW YORK: I asked a guy in a Jeep to take me to the *Daily News* and he did. There wasn't even a question in my mind that we'd lost people. When I got there, I said, "I need to know who's dead. Who didn't get out?" It was unbelievable that we had seven photographers down there and none died.

I approved more than 100 pictures for (editors) to look at. I gave them a wide variety of choices. It was the whole narrative of the story up to that moment, with the exception of one picture of the fireball coming down the street, which I didn't take. It's hard to say now because I'm alive, but I'll always wonder if I would have been able to make that picture.

> ‘ I need to know who's dead. Who didn't get out? ’

MARTIN WOLK | Business Reporter
MSNBC.com

NEW YORK: I tried to call my boss in Redmond, Washington. It was impossible. My mother has a personal toll-free number in Cleveland. I got her. She called my boss on her other line, then she held the two phones together and I dictated my story.

ADAM LISBERG | Staff Writer
The Record, Hackensack, N.J.

NEW YORK: For a while it was eerily quiet, just the thrum of engines and water. Paramedics were scavenging materials from ambulances. There were a couple of photographers. I only recognized Todd Maisel, the *Daily News* photographer. He's your stereotypical, city, breaking-news reporter, Army jacket on. He was standing there crying. I put my hand on his shoulder. "Hey man, it's OK. It's OK," I said. Another photographer said, "Hey man, put that gear to work. Get to work. Think about history now." I felt so naked. They had cameras. I didn't.

> ' I felt so naked. They had cameras. I didn't. '

New York *Daily News* photographer Todd Maisel at the site of the World Trade Center disaster.

Robert Mecea

NAOMI HALPERIN | Photo Editor
The Morning Call, Allentown, Pa.

ALLENTOWN, Pa.: Between 10 a.m. and our deadline at 2 p.m. — the special edition hit the street at 3:30 p.m. — all I was looking at were pictures. As a picture editor, I'm looking at each picture, frame by still frame. That does something completely different to you. We cleared off a newsroom wall and put up hundreds of photos. People were coming in, tourists from New York City with photos. We're only one and a half hours from Manhattan. So we lined the walls. I liked doing it that way to give me an instant "gut-check." I can hear reactions from people walking through the newsroom. When you edit pictures, you try to get the ultimate in storytelling. You have the most tragic event of American history. You, as a newspaper, have a responsibility to tell the truth, to be accurate, to make sure you do justice to the history of it.

> When you edit pictures, you try to get the ultimate in storytelling.

NANCY GABRINER | Editorial Producer
ABC News

NEW YORK: I sit next to Peter (Jennings) and write him notes. The only voice in his ear is that of Marc Burstein, executive producer for special events. That day, Marc and someone else were going to London for meetings. Marc was at the airport, about to get on a flight to London, when he heard. He ended up commandeering a taxi and somehow getting back into the city. By showing his New York City police press pass, he got in.

Marc tries to speak in Peter's ear as little as possible. Marc will tell me that these are the correspondents available, and I write that on a card. Peter will decide whom to speak to. Peter has the menu of people he can call in front of him on a piece of paper. His ability to look at a piece of paper, absorb it, keep speaking and understand is amazing. It's a God-given talent. I work with other anchorpeople when he's not here, and it can be a very big distraction for someone else. But he can do it. I know not to distract him midthought.

ROBERT A. CUMINS | Documentary Photographer
Black Star

NEW YORK: I wonder if I got that fireball on film and decide I'd better get going. I go to the lab. The first thing I see is that the processing machine is completely apart. I ask, "How long until this is fixed?" I need to get this processed. There's a CVS drugstore next door, so I take it over. As a professional, I never take film to get developed at CVS, but it's the same developer to a degree. I figure if they screw it up, I didn't lose anything because the whole world was getting it on film that day. I'm rushing them, saying, "I need it really quick." She puts it right in. I'm pacing. Finally it comes out, and I see images on it. She asks, "What's on this thing, anyway?" I say, "Trade Center."

I take the film, bring it to the lab, and we put it in the scanner. We get a series of thumbnails on the scanner like a contact sheet on the monitor. I see a total of 19 frames. My eyes went to the center because I had a sense that I had been shooting before I saw the fireball. I'm a little confused and say, "Bring them up one at a time." He brought up the first frame — 00A — that's the picture of the plane just before impact. The second picture is the tail of the airplane sticking out of the building, a millionth of a second before it exploded. The third is the fireball. I went, "Oh my God! I remember that plane! I followed it right into the building!"

> I was almost in midreport to CNBC when the tower collapsed, and they probably figured I was dead.

JOHN BUSSEY | Foreign Editor
The Wall Street Journal

NEW YORK: Boats were putting in at the river, ferrying people across to Liberty State Park in Jersey City. I got a quarter and started using the telephone. I called in because I was almost in midreport to CNBC when the tower collapsed, and they probably figured I was dead. Then I started calling colleagues to find out who made it out. There was this very intense period at the *Journal* where we just didn't know how each other was. I did a couple of paragraphs for our story that night and asked somebody to call my relatives.

BOLÍVAR ARELLANO | Photographer
New York Post

NEW YORK: I went back to the paper, and everyone was surprised to see me. I said I didn't want to lose my film, I wanted to develop it. My son, who is a photo editor at the *New York Post* — he's my boss — said, "What are you doing here, Poppy? No, no, Poppy, I will develop your film." I left five films on the table. Because so many people were coming to the paper with pictures — free-lance and professional — I lost one roll I left on the table. I lost (another) roll and my cell phone when I went flying in (the collapse of) Tower One. My son threw me out of the paper and sent me to the hospital. They put five stitches in my right knee.

DOUG FEAVER | Executive Editor and Vice President
Washingtonpost.com

ARLINGTON, Va.: By noon we needed to make the home page fast and light. The more we had on a page, the bigger the load on our server and the greater the chance of it crashing. We decided to strip the page down to just this story. No weather. No traffic. All the other Internet sites did the same thing. We were all getting hammered.

> We decided to strip the page down to just this story.

CRAIG COLA | Photographer
Washingtonpost.com

ARLINGTON, Va.: There were probably 25 people on top of the Pentagon City mall garage watching, so I set the video camera on a tripod and acted as a reporter. I was waiting for a runner in a car to get my tapes for the Web site, but by then traffic was insane. I gave up and started driving back myself. I got stuck in traffic. I talked to my assignment editor and said, "I can't do anything." He was at home and said he'd get his bike, come to me and ride it to the office. He came running down the street on his bike. I flagged him down and handed him one tape. I didn't even pull over.

MOLLY RILEY | News Assistant
Reuters

> All I'm thinking is, 'Where can I get the best shot with the camera I have?'

ARLINGTON, Va.: All I'm thinking is, "Where can I get the best shot with the camera I have?" That was OK because with smoke and flames still coming out of windows, I didn't need a zoom. Because we are a wire service, we take handouts from military photographers. Because I didn't have the equipment to make better close-ups, I asked other photographers there if they'd shoot for us. One military photographer later e-mailed me several photos. I was still pretty far. I was to the left in front of the helipad. I waited there, looking for different things to happen. Then I climbed up on Interstate 395 so I could get a picture of the Pentagon exit sign. I was running out of pictures. I had a digital card, and it had a finite number. I needed to transmit the photos. I rode my bike back home.

Rescue workers respond to the crash of a hijacked aircraft at the Pentagon while smoke billows from the building.

Molly Riley/Reuters

12:29

Betsy Steuart Cunningham | Producer
NBC News

WASHINGTON: I started walking with some colleagues from Fox and CNN toward the National Press Building, which is on the other side of the White House from the State Department. We were hearing that streets were closed off. One of my colleagues was not in the kind of shoes that you should walk multiple blocks in. We got to about 20th and Pennsylvania N.W., and there was (Hearst Newspapers columnist) Helen Thomas and some of the White House press corps, sort of holding forth on the street. People came up to her because she is a well-known journalist, and she was telling them what she knew.

We had to go far out of our way and make a U-turn around the White House to get down to the (National) Press Building. We were trying to make phone calls, trying to reach the State Department spokesman. At that point, everybody was just pooling resources. If somebody had a cell phone number for someone that somebody else didn't have, they would make the phone call. We were trying to work as we went. At one point, we found another group of White House reporters who had been kicked out of the White House when it was evacuated. They had no place to go.

My colleague's feet were hurting so much from her high heels that a passer-by offered her a pair of gym socks. As we walked, people were helping people, sharing water and information. We were telling people, "No, there is no car bomb at the State Department."

> As we walked, people were helping people, sharing water and information.

Beth Fertig | Reporter
WNYC Radio

NEW YORK: We were able to feed our tape to NPR (National Public Radio) and to our station. NPR didn't have many people on the ground in New York. It was basically left to us to be NPR's reporters that day.

LISA BURGESS | Pentagon Reporter
Stars and Stripes

ARLINGTON, Va.: One of the guys that I helped in the court-yard was in one of the offices that had blown up. He was shell-shocked and bleeding from the head. He was not panicky. He kept saying that there was a bomb in the Xerox machine. He was a Vietnam vet. He was absolutely convinced the entire episode originated from his office. The Xerox blew up and so did the woman standing next to it, he said. If the violence of the explosion led him to believe that there was a bomb in the same room, that gives you a sense of what the noise was.

We saw people half-carried by other people. They were gravely injured. One poor guy was sitting on the lawn. His entire face was burned. His arms were so badly burned that the medical technician was trying desperately to find a vein to get an IV in. The impact was so great that it blew people's clothes off. The Xerox bomb guy came in to work wearing dress pants, a tie and button-down shirt. He had his shoes, shirt and tie blown off his body. There were shreds of them. If you looked at the rags of this burned guy, you could see the extent of the charring to the clothes. It made your blood run cold. But there weren't hundreds streaming out like this.

> He had his shoes, shirt and tie blown off his body.

ARTHUR SANTANA | D.C. Superior Court Reporter
The Washington Post

ARLINGTON, Va.: I ended up in this "walking wounded" area on the Potomac River side of the Pentagon. I was in a triage area. Wounded people were still walking out. I was without a camera and had my note pad tucked in my pocket, so I didn't get pushed out. The next thing I know, I was roped into help-ing. I started moving oxygen tanks for patients, handing out latex gloves and surgeons' masks. They put me behind a cart with medical supplies. We pushed this medical cart into the center of the Pentagon courtyard, where I stayed for the first couple of hours. I called the desk. I kept trying. Busy signal.

The city desk editor, Gabe Escobar, said, "Where are you?" I said, "I'm in the courtyard of the Pentagon." He thought I was at the courthouse. I'm screaming, "No, courtyard!" It shocked him as much as it shocked me that I was there. Gabe immediately patched me through to the reporter taking feeds.

At one point early in the courtyard, it just so happened that there was an Army public information person. I don't know him. I don't cover the Pentagon. I identified myself: "Here's my card," I told him. I just got roped into this, and I'd rather observe. I was worried I would get kicked out. He said, "Look, Arthur, I've seen you've been helping out. It's fine for you to stick around."

Going into it, I was a reporter. But by the time I found myself going into the courtyard of the Pentagon, I think I became a person helping out and not a reporter. When I was in the courtyard, and there came a time when it got slow, I reverted back to my role as a reporter. I thought I needed to identify myself, and I did. I was happy I did when he said I could stay. It seemed inappropriate to take out my notebook and interview a firefighter. It seemed the right thing to do was to hand him a bottle of water rather than stick a note pad in his face.

> ❛ I became a person helping out and not a reporter. ❜

A Pentagon employee receives aid after a hijacked aircraft crashed into the building.

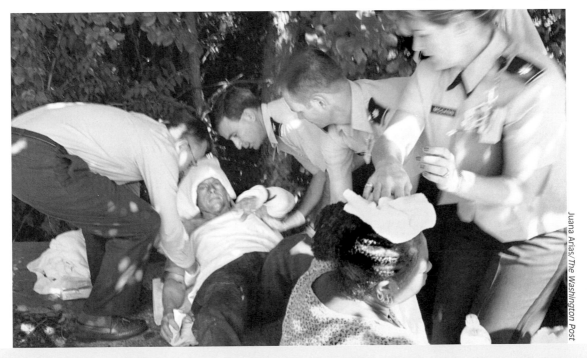

Juana Arias/The Washington Post

DAVE STATTER | Reporter
WUSA

ARLINGTON, Va.: I was a volunteer firefighter years ago and learned something there. You have to remain calm and size up what's before you. About 39 minutes into the incident, the collapse occurred. We were actually live on the air — all five floors tumbling into each other and onto the ground. A few minutes later, they moved us back.

We try as much as possible — and it was difficult during the initial stages of this — to get all information back to the reporters before they put it on the air. AP ran a story of a State Department bombing. A lot of news organizations, including ours, put that on the air. But from my location, I couldn't verify, so I didn't report it.

We talked very early on (about) a lot of rumors that you're going to hear throughout the day and a lot of things that won't be true. Our job is to ferret out, try to figure out what is true and what is not.

> Our job is to ferret out, try to figure out what is true and what is not.

DAVE WINSLOW | Correspondent
The Associated Press

ARLINGTON, Va.: When I was on air, I was just reporting what I was seeing from my apartment. I don't know why I wasn't at all excited. I've heard my tape. I almost sound matter-of-fact. I was trying to describe what I saw and what was happening around me where the attack had taken place. While I was on air, there was another loud boom, a second explosion occurred which I described.

I just knew we were under attack. I had a choice — either stay where I was or leave the building and run to the Pentagon. I have a view of all of Washington, the Capitol, Washington Monument, State Department. I knew AP would send people over to the Pentagon. I stayed put, feeling I could serve more knowledgeably from where I was. During all this, my stomach went into a knot. Bombs were falling out of the sky. I know what the people in the (World War II) London bombing felt. I'm 54 and never felt anything like that in the United States. The only time I remember ever feeling that lack of control was in the 1962 Cuban missile crisis.

My girlfriend (in North Carolina) was scared. She couldn't get through. A friend of hers in the office turned on the local 50,000-watt AM radio station in the Raleigh-Durham market. She heard me describing it live and knew I was OK.

ELINOR TATUM | Publisher and Editor in Chief
New York Amsterdam News

NEW YORK: My staff was getting increasingly nervous about noon. At that point, one of my free-lancers came in on his bike. He had ridden from Harlem all the way down to get more photographs and stories. People were calling with photographs. All of a sudden there were a million photographers in New York. You don't understand how many people I had to turn down, at least 20. We paid our going rate for photos. I wasn't about to be yanked. The front page was almost all photos.

> All of a sudden there were a million photographers in New York.

JOHN CARROLL | Editor and Executive Vice President
Los Angeles Times

LOS ANGELES: Before noon, I started working to get a chartered airplane to get to New York. We had seven people in our New York City bureau. We had two (other) people in town, fashion writers, normally in L.A. but who were in New York for Fashion Week. We also had a sportswriter there, but we knew we needed more. We chartered a Gulfstream II, a jet. We just did what we thought we had to do, and nobody ever thought to second-guess us. We did that right away but were unable to get it off the ground until Thursday because of the restrictions. So Thursday we got 12 people on that Gulfstream and landed at Teterboro Airport in New Jersey.

HOWELL RAINES

NEW YORK: I came out of a noon meeting and saw a group of photographers standing around (*Times* photographer) Ruth Fremson. They were pulling debris out of her hair. She was in the street when one of the towers collapsed. She raced down the street with a cloud of debris rolling behind her. She took a memorable photograph of a policeman bending over, catching his breath. He had pulled Ruth into the deli. I was terribly worried about our staff. When I saw Ruth and heard her story, I realized how dangerous it was for our staff at any given moment. Being chosen to lead a staff of 1,037 is a heavy responsibility.

MAGGIE FARLEY

NEW YORK: I stopped by New York's oldest mosque in the neighborhood and asked to interview the imam (Muslim prayer leader). They told me to come back for noon prayers. At noon, I went to the mosque. There was a Muslim covered with ash who worked at Merrill Lynch. He was finishing his ritual ablutions before the noon prayer. He was very angry I was there. "You are assuming that a Muslim did this. Why are you here?" he said.

I was there because the police were there, and I was wondering if they were worried about a backlash. They also were victims of what had happened, and I wanted to hear what the imam had to say. Someone led him away.

I stayed by the doorway, and someone translated the lesson or sermon. I talked to the imam afterward. He's from Egypt, and he gave a very peaceful message: What had happened today is against Islam, and everybody should go out and donate blood.

I would go home periodically and call in or file by computer on the DSL. Cell phones were a letdown, but the BlackBerry was the hero.

AARON BROWN | Anchor
CNN

NEW YORK: One thing for me, because I tend to be conservative in these things, is I don't ever want to be ahead of the story. If I had to do it again, about 30 minutes before I actually said those words, 'The United States of America is under attack,' I would have said those words. I thought I was a little late in saying them. Those are really hard words to say. You never, or I had never in my life, thought that I would someday utter that sentence. It's a very hard sentence to say. It's not one that rolls easily off your tongue.

> ' The United States of America is under attack. '

A firefighter pauses on a bench as he works in Lower Manhattan at the scene of the World Trade Center terrorist attacks.

Matt Moyer/The Associated Press

3:25   3:26   3:27

3:28 P.M. CNN: NEW YORK — GIULIANI SAYS PUBLIC TRANSPORTATION IS RESTORED.

ABC NEWS

SPECIAL REPORT: AMERICA UNDER ATTACK

Ann Compton: *"The president has just made a statement, Peter, a very emotional one, saying that freedom has been attacked but freedom will be defended, saying that America's military is on its highest state of alert."*

PAUL STEIGER | Managing Editor
The Wall Street Journal

NEW YORK: I realize I'm wearing my best blue suit and I'm totally white, covered with ash. I'm walking out on the street where there's nobody else like me. I go to the building, and the doorman says, "Are you all right?" I get to my apartment and track down my wife through the BlackBerry. It turns out she's fine.

I called (deputy managing editor) Barney Calame, and he says, "Is this Paul Steiger?" And I say, "Yeah." And I realize he's choking up. I suddenly realized people were worried about me. I discovered that we have the beginnings of a production set up in South Brunswick (N.J.). Jim Pensiero was there, he's putting together an editing desk; the two Larrys (Rout and Ingrassia) are there; Washington is putting together a great sked (schedule of news stories). I also discover that all of the senior editors are stuck in Manhattan, or in the case of Marcus Brauchli, the national (news) editor, in Brooklyn.

Later, I discovered that (*Journal* reporters and editors) have great stories going. Bryan Gruley, a Washington editor, has 600 inches of great, eyewitness stuff to do a scope-of-the-devastation piece.

> ❛ I suddenly realized people were worried about me. ❜

MARCUS BRAUCHLI | National News Editor
The Wall Street Journal

NEW YORK: I began cobbling together the next day's story list, helped in large part by what Washington bureau chief Alan Murray already had done and by the assignments I was making. By midday, we had a list of stories that I sent to all bureaus and to South Brunswick (N.J.), so the team that arrived there would know what was coming.

CAROL MARIN | Contributor
CBS News

NEW YORK: I figured I'd hitchhike back up the West Side Highway when I see all these firefighters yelling, "Run! The gas main is going to blow!" I banged on an emergency vehicle and asked them if they would carry me as far as they would. I got as far as 42nd Street, where I saw an empty New York City bus. I tapped on the door and asked if I could ride as far as they were going. The driver said, "I'll take you where you are going." He dropped me off at Studio 47 at 524 West 57th Street, where Dan Rather was broadcasting. Ten minutes after I walked into the studio, I was on the air. Somebody took me over to the anchor desk and wired me up with a mike and an IFB, the thing you put in your ear to hear off the air. I said to Dan, "I was saved by a firefighter."

> I was saved by a firefighter.

DAN RATHER | Anchor and Managing Editor
CBS News

NEW YORK: Once you are in the cocoon, nothing breaks it. It's almost hermetically sealed. Remember when Carol Marin came to the studio? She was inside the cocoon. I've known Carol for a long time. She's a very experienced reporter. She was obviously shaken. That's understandable. So, these things tick off in your mind.

It's Carol. She's really shook up. I've got to get the best out of her. What's the best way to get the best out of her? Try to make her feel comfortable. Try to settle her down. Try to make her feel protected. I don't mean to sound patronizing. Maybe she needs to feel the warmth of a human hand.

To be a good anchor, by my definition, you must be passionately engaged in the responsibility of what you are doing. We have to be good. It's a huge story. Besides that, you have to have an awareness that people — especially on the West Coast — are going to be turning to the set at different times.

STEPHEN LUCAS | Director
"Today in New York," WNBC News

NEW YORK: My job at this point is to focus on what's happening in front of us, to get information to the viewer and let them know what's happening. Whether we're going to stay live or we're going to give it back to the network is passed on to me through the producer. At that point, my concern is trying to stay with pictures that are going to make sense with whatever the talent's talking about at that time. Once everything was up and going, I had 30 sources coming in at a time.

WILLIAM F. BAKER | President and CEO
Thirteen/WNET New York

NEW YORK: One of our producers said the World Trade Center was the center of emergency activity for New York City, and the Office of Emergency Management couldn't function. We offered Channel 13's resources. We have the biggest phone banks in New York and the capability of working with hundreds of volunteers, along with a big computer support system. So 300 people from the Red Cross moved up here (West 33rd Street) and set up tables in our hallways. The Office of Emergency Management used our boardroom as its center. Our telephone numbers were given out over radio and TV stations to tell people trying to find loved ones to call the Red Cross at this number. People didn't realize they were calling the pledge number at Channel 13.

> People from the Red Cross moved up here and set up tables in our hallways.

PAUL STEIGER, NEW YORK: We're thinking, "How do we get to South Brunswick?" I try to get a rental car, but there are none. I try to get a radio car; there are none. One of my deputies keeps a car near Columbia Presbyterian Hospital. He takes the subway to his car and starts to drive down. He bangs into a truck in front of him, and his radiator explodes.

> I try to get a rental car, but there are none.

Meantime, I'm talking to another colleague. He is monitoring the radio and discovers that traffic is horrible, the George Washington Bridge is open only intermittently, the tunnels are closed. I figured that all of the deputy managing editors live within walking distance of each other. I'm the only one on the East Side. So I said to Barney (Calame), "Let's use your apartment as a staging area."

From Barney's apartment we start reading copy. It's all being edited and put in the paper by these fantastic people in South Brunswick, New Jersey. The reason we're able to do this is because South Brunswick is a second pagination site for us. We normally do the (financial) tables in South Brunswick and

The Wall Street Journal broke with tradition on September 12 and published its first six-column headline since World War II to emphasize the magnitude of the attacks on the United States.

THE WALL STREET JOURNAL.

© 2001 Dow Jones & Company, Inc. All Rights Reserved.

DOWJONES   VOL. CCXXXVIII NO. 51   EE/PR ★★★★   WEDNESDAY, SEPTEMBER 12, 2001   WSJ.com $1.00

TERRORISTS DESTROY WORLD TRADE CENTER, HIT PENTAGON IN RAID WITH HIJACKED JETS

Nation Stands In Disbelief And Horror

Streets of Manhattan Resemble War Zone Amid Clouds of Ash

What's News—

Business and Finance

World-Wide

Death Toll, Source of Devastating Attacks Remain Unclear; U.S. Vows Retaliation as Attention Focuses on bin Laden

Hour of Horror Forever Alters American Lives

the rest of the paper out of New York. They can just expand the South Brunswick pagination system to do the whole paper there. I said I wanted a six-column headline on Page One, which we very rarely do. We wrote the head. I don't remember what it said. They humored me and said they liked mine the best, so that's the one we went with.

JESSE LEWIS | National Copy Chief
The Wall Street Journal

NEW YORK: We did a six-column headline. My thought is that's reserved for the end of the world. That was close to it. It was, I'm told, the only six-column we've done since World War II. It's the biggest I've ever seen here, and I've been here almost 15 years.

JIM PENSIERO | Assistant Managing Editor
The Wall Street Journal

SOUTH BRUNSWICK, N.J.: I sent around to all bureaus the size paper we were going to try for and the deadline we were going to shoot for. We were going to shoot for an 8:30 p.m. lockup, which is about an hour later than normal. In talking to production and circulation, we felt we could get our papers delivered if we could lock it up by then, and update as needed.

ROBERT J. HUGHES | Reporter
The Wall Street Journal

NEW YORK: I started walking along the Bowery, stopped in one of the missions and got some water. I walked about eight miles. I stopped at an office in midtown to try to call my mother. I have 10 brothers and sisters, and a couple work in the area. Everyone was OK.

I got home about 3:30 p.m., logged on to the computer and got my editor on the phone. I broke down. I felt very embarrassed. He said, "You were the last reporter to check in."

> It was ... the only six-column we've done since World War II.

CATHERINE LEUTHOLD | Photographer
Free-lance

NEW YORK: Around 1 p.m., that's when cops and firemen were starting to get angry and saying we had to leave. Finally, I couldn't take it any longer. I felt so heavy. I had tried making phone calls, and there were no phones. I couldn't call anyone. It didn't matter. I didn't remember phone numbers.

I went over to the Brooklyn Bridge and did an overview. I looked back and took pictures of down below the FDR Drive with no one on it. I got people still coming over and totally in shock. Then I slowly walked out to my lab.

It fascinated me that there were so many women photographers involved. They stayed. They were incredibly strong and purposeful in what they took pictures of. What I really respect about all the journalists there is that they put together pieces of the puzzle. There wasn't an overall picture story. Each person told a part of the story. I told the East Side and North Side story. There was the South Side story. To me, all the photos from different angles tell the story. It was never one photo that told the whole story.

> There were no phones. It didn't matter. I didn't remember phone numbers.

The view from the Brooklyn Bridge of the deserted FDR Drive several hours after the attack.

Catherine Leuthold

Adam Lisberg | Staff Writer
The Record, Hackensack, N.J.

NEW YORK: I'm watching firefighters clambering up a pile and wishing to high hell I had my cameras with me. I'm thinking this is a story you tell in pictures, not words. I remembered the grocery store around the corner. It's abandoned. People had looted water from the front cases. I got some Pop-Tarts. I'm starving, but that was the least of my worries at this point. In the front of the store, they had cheap disposable cameras. There were some that were actual cameras. Price tag was $19.99. I felt bad taking it and would have paid the guy. I felt less bad when I went in and there were two cops taking cameras off the wall, trying to figure out how to put the film in. I showed them and said, "Never think a reporter never did anything for a cop."

I went back to the corner, pointed and shot. There's a saying in photography: F8 and be there. That was the case. One picture I took shows four or five firemen, so you can see these three pieces of façade that have speared into the ground. In front is a cab of the fire engine. Whatever is behind them has been crushed.

> ❛ I'm thinking this is a story you tell in pictures, not words. ❜

Firefighters search debris, dwarfed by the shards of the collapsed World Trade Center on September 11.

Adam Lisberg/The Record (Bergen County, N.J.)

> I hand it to Peter, and the look on his face is, 'You want me to report this?' And I nod back.

NANCY GABRINER | Editorial Producer
ABC News

NEW YORK: Obviously it was a very upsetting day, but I don't think I externally displayed my nerves. I was actually shaking part of the day. The truth is there were not many moments when I could think about what was happening. The thing I worry about most is giving Peter (Jennings) wrong information. I remember when someone gave me some reporting from Lisa Stark. She was able to confirm that the two planes were commercial. I remember whispering, "Is she sure this is right?" They nod. I hand it to Peter, and the look on his face is, "You want me to report this?" And I nod back.

PETER JENNINGS | Anchor and Senior Editor
ABC News

NEW YORK: My job is to listen to everybody, question everybody and try to build as complete and as comprehensive a picture as I can. I get a constant stream of information in my ear, a constant stream of information and advice from Nancy (Gabriner). People are filing on the ABC urgent news wire. One of the things that helps is that I know all our people well. One of the very first people I spoke with was Lisa Stark, who covers aviation. She has superb sources. Suddenly she, then somebody else and somebody else all appear on my radar. Suddenly it's like being an air traffic controller.

MARK STENCEL | Vice President, Multimedia and Global Ventures
Washingtonpost.com

ARLINGTON, Va.: Until now, video and multimedia had fallen into the bells-and-whistles category (on Web sites). We saw so much use of video that day. We have televisions but people were watching on streaming video. The story was very visual. We served more than 12,000 hours of streaming content on September 11, which is unparalleled.

AARON BROWN | Anchor
CNN

NEW YORK: (My producer) David (Bohrman) and I think we both share a brain sometimes. He knows what I need and what I don't need. And when you are in that kind of situation, what you don't need is as important as what you do. What you don't want is someone talking to you all the time. Most of these people were absolutely new to me. I've never met them. In some cases I did not know their names. I've apologized, I think, to half the organization for mispronouncing names at various points.

It was a terrible setup (broadcasting from the top of CNN's roof), but the roof was the perfect place to do it. The monitors didn't work very well. Half the time I couldn't hear. A lot of the time I couldn't see the monitors. But I know I said to the viewers very often during the day, "You can probably see things more clearly than I."

> You can probably see things more clearly than I.

DAN FROOMKIN | Managing Editor
Washingtonpost.com

ARLINGTON, Va.: We were having a really hard time updating the story on President Bush. One hour after the second press conference, we still had the first story up. Our entire dynamic publishing system crashed not long after the planes. The site didn't go down. The public didn't know because we did an amazing job of hiding our failure.

HOWARD PARNELL | Managing Editor,
Local News and Community Development
Washingtonpost.com

ARLINGTON, Va.: Things are in motion. What can the Web add? By midday we decided to ask for reactions to what was happening by e-mail. We had hundreds and hundreds come in. By 3 p.m., we were getting three or four a minute.

LISA BURGESS | Pentagon Reporter
Stars and Stripes

ARLINGTON, Va.: Later, we went back to the courtyard (at the Pentagon). There were close to 100 people. Some were setting up triage teams. One problem with the Pentagon is there are so many damn officers. Everyone wanted to be in charge. It was a case of too many chiefs and not enough Indians. There also was a problem with firemen getting water on the fire. One of the water mains in the basement was broken. Everybody was anxious to go in and look for survivors, but they couldn't go in because of smoke and heat.

ARTHUR SANTANA | D.C. Superior Court Reporter
The Washington Post

> One military guy corralled several people to prepare for body recovery duty. I got in that line.

ARLINGTON, Va.: During the early stage, one military guy corralled several people to prepare for body recovery duty. I got in that line. We had latex gloves, surgeon masks and were in line. We established a buddy to go in with. They called it off. There was too much smoke. Later, I was in body recovery duty again. I got the corner of a gurney, four people assigned to a gurney. We wore gloves and masks. We were ready to go in. We were near this makeshift morgue area, but it didn't happen. Still too much smoke.

GREG EDWARDS | Reporter
Richmond (Va.) Times-Dispatch

ARLINGTON, Va.: A photographer and I were on Interstate 95 about a half-hour north of Richmond when we heard of the Pentagon attack on the car radio and decided to change plans and head for Arlington. By the time I got to Interstate 395, the smoke coming out of the building had died down, but there was still a lot of confusion and activity. A group of people was gathered along the interstate, watching the building burn. I soaked in the scene and looked for people to talk with. The place felt dangerous.

JIM LO SCALZO | Photographer
U.S. News & World Report

ARLINGTON, Va.: About 2 p.m., I said, "Screw this, I'm going to go to the Pentagon." I took the Metro to Pentagon City. Lugging all this equipment, I ran down Interstate 395 and hopped a few fences. I didn't try to get close; every policeman and his brother were there. Trying to get up high, I ran across the street to the Navy Annex. I got there about 3 p.m. The sun was in the west. You could see the Capitol dome through the smoke.

I didn't take many shots, maybe two or three rolls. I was there a half-hour when I got a page that the president was coming back. Oh shit, I was in the wrong place. The press pool was gathering at the FBI (headquarters). I ran and found a cab. There were three Japanese men with video cameras in the cab. They'd gone to do some videoing. They couldn't decide what to do. I was standing there trying to be patient. But I really needed to get to the FBI. I wasn't even supposed to be at the Pentagon. I finally yelled, "Are you f-----g staying or going?" They jumped out, and I got in. I got really lucky. I got back in the pool just in time to go over to the White House and wait for the president.

> ' You could see the Capitol dome through the smoke. '

Jim Lo Scalzo/U.S. News & World Report

Smoke from the Pentagon obscures the view of the U.S. Capitol.

JOAN ROSEN | New York State Photo Editor
The Associated Press

NEW YORK: I remember looking over (Richard) Drew's shoulder as he edited pictures. He wanted to move more pictures of the burning buildings. I had already seen a hundred pictures of the burning buildings. He told me people were jumping out of the buildings. I said, "That's what I want to see. You've got to move that stuff now!"

I was so emotionally removed from it. You have a camera and a viewfinder, and it puts something between you and the subject. I'm looking for the best photo, the best composition, drama. It was not until much later that it occurred to me what I'd been looking at — people who were dying. It still bothers me that I didn't feel that at first.

I know that newspapers do have a responsibility to their community, but they also have a responsibility to tell the story — and this was part of the story.

> ❝ I was so emotionally removed from it. ❞

Reporters, photographers and photo editors working at the New York City bureau of The Associated Press on September 11. Joan Rosen, the New York state photo editor, can be seen at back left, on the phone.

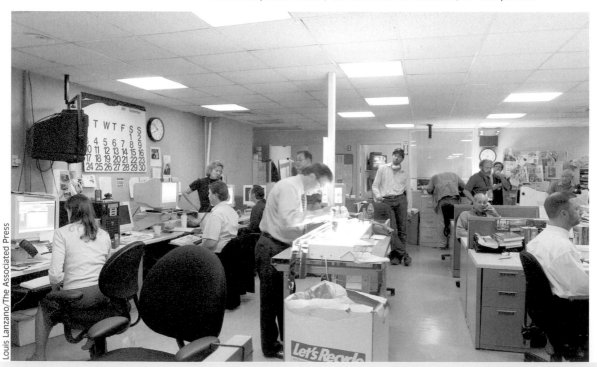

Louis Lanzano/The Associated Press

4:10 P.M. CNN — BUILDING 7 OF THE WORLD TRADE CENTER COMPLEX IS REPORTED ON FIRE.

RICHARD DREW | Photographer
The Associated Press

NEW YORK: I was in the kitchen of the Ambassador Hotel in Los Angeles when Robert Kennedy was killed (in June 1968). You see 5,000 people die at once, or you see one person die. We record history every day. My picture of the man falling was a part of history. We are visual journalists who record history.

NAOMI HALPERIN | Photo Editor
The Morning Call, Allentown, Pa.

ALLENTOWN, Pa.: I saw it (Drew's photo of a man jumping) as soon as it moved in the early afternoon. Up to this point, every photo was about twisted metal and broken buildings and people running. Without the photo, you cannot say visually that this is a horrific loss of life. To hide that photo would be to hide that truth. What I was struck by with this photo was the position of this man. Did he jump or fall?

I look at it and see that he jumped. He made a choice in a situation where there weren't many choices left. I saw that in his body language. We probably ran that photo bigger than anyone in the country, tip to stern on the broadsheet (full page). He was everybody who died. It was a flash-point image — the point you realize there's a severe loss of life. The photo has depth. To run it that tall gave it the tower feeling. If I had to do it again, I'd do it in a heartbeat.

> To hide that photo (of a man jumping) would be to hide that truth.

PETER JENNINGS, NEW YORK: We didn't have any videotape of the jumpers but were aware it was occurring. We made an early decision not to put jumpers on. At the time, it was too painful.

It's a good question in retrospect. I did recall a previous occasion where there was a hotel fire in Taiwan. We actually (showed footage of) people jumping out of the buildings. The Taiwan coverage didn't receive criticism, I suppose, because it was far away.

TOM FRANKLIN | Photographer
The Record, Hackensack, N.J.

> ❝ They kept trying to push us out, but most journalists were pretty determined that day. ❞

JERSEY CITY, N.J.: My assignment was to go to Jersey City, on the New Jersey side of the Hudson River, just across the river from Lower Manhattan. It was pretty dramatic there because you could see the whole thing unfold. They had a triage center and were bringing a lot of the injured over on boats. While I was there, police were really in a panic trying to keep everyone away from the riverfront because they were evacuating that area. A couple of photojournalists and myself were pretty persistent in trying to stay. They kept trying to push us out, but most journalists were pretty determined that day.

Sometime around 2:30 p.m., John Wheeler, who is another photographer, and I got on a boat, and they took us to Lower Manhattan. I owe that all to John Wheeler, a free-lance photographer. He said, "I think I know the police official here. I think we can get on a boat." They weren't crazy about us getting off the boat, but you know, this story had to be documented. The tugboat captain gave us water and masks to wear. They dropped us off at the World Financial Center, which was fortunate for us, because that was right where we needed to be. I think a lot of other journalists in Manhattan probably had to evacuate the area for their own safety or because of police

Photographer Tom Franklin of *The Record* at the World Trade Center site.

John W. Wheeler

and rescue concerns. We came in the backdoor and got right to Ground Zero. Getting pictures and recording this was the goal. I had never felt such a strong desire to reach that goal as I did that day.

JOHN DEL GIORNO | Helicopter Reporter
Metro Networks/
Shadow Broadcasting, WABC-TV

NEW YORK: We stayed out there until almost 2 o'clock. They canceled clearances one by one. They'd say, "OK, that's a news helicopter, tell him to land. That's another news helicopter, tell him to land." Nobody was happier to get back on the ground than we were because we had just seen what was really a war zone. My pilot, a Vietnam veteran pilot, said to me, "I've seen jungles turn to green mist, but I've never seen stuff like this."

> We had just seen what was really a war zone.

MAGGIE FARLEY | Bureau Chief, U.N./Canada
Los Angeles Times

NEW YORK: I went to the hospital nearby. Three carloads of plainclothes police pulled up, jumped out and put on bullet-proof vests, and I ran after them. A policeman said they had a report that a car with a bomb had gone into the emergency room at NYU Hospital, so police were going to all emergency rooms. I called the office. We had reporters sitting by police scanners. John Goldman, who is senior correspondent, has been preparing for something like this since the '93 Trade Center bombing when he was running the bureau. He outfitted the office with police scanners and an emergency plan for covering terrorism. He had us all outfitted with police passes. John Goldman was listening to the police scanner. He said, "I just sent a reporter to NYU Hospital because of the victims." That was the last time I was able to make phone contact with the office. I never knew that the ER story was not true until the next day.

RACHEL R. SNYDER | Staff Reporter
Daily Courier, Connellsville, Pa.

SHANKSVILLE, Pa.: There was a bystander (Mark Stahl) who saw the plane go down and got pictures before police and firemen arrived. He just happened to have a digital camera with him. He was gone before any media people came to the site, but came back with the pictures developed and printed. That was the first viewing most of the media got of the crash site. The media were lined up, and people started running after this guy down this dirt road. I was out of breath. In fact, I was running so hard I actually lost my pager clipped to my side. I did not know why I was running. But I knew there must be something big.

His wife and kids were in the Jeep. He opened his door and stepped out. That was as far as he could go. He was surrounded by media. People were shouting at him, "Can you point the picture in this direction? Can you explain what's in the picture? Can you hold it up higher?" I can't believe he could even understand the questions, there was such mass chaos.

> That was the first viewing most of the media got of the crash site.

KEITH SRAKOCIC | Staff Photographer
The Associated Press

SHANKSVILLE, Pa.: This guy (Mark Stahl) comes in his four-wheel-drive vehicle. It was close to 2 or 3 p.m. when he showed up with those photos. He drives into the parking area where we all parked. There's whispering, "He's got pictures of the crash." My goal is twofold — to photograph what's going on and to see if the AP may be interested in the pictures. I told him whom I was with. I told him these pictures are going to be seen on the wire and that somebody would get in touch with him to purchase rights.

Everybody was very civilized. He held them up nicely, and people were looking at them. I was basically trying to shoot pictures. The reporters were trying to get a time frame, whether he saw the crash and where it hit. Once I felt I had a picture we could use with him in it, I tried to get his name and phone number. They were swarming around him. As the crowd started to gather, he moved up the road another 200 feet, and everyone started running after him. People were talking about acquiring his pictures. Actually, I've seen media behave much worse.

Later, we hopped on what I would describe as a tour bus. It took media to this vantage point, about a half mile from the crash site. You saw police and military personnel around the perimeter. The crash site scene was not much to see, a crater basically. I remember peering through my long lens to see if I could see anything in the woods behind it. It seemed like they put us on the bus quicker than I wanted to get on. We got back, and (Pennsylvania) Gov. Tom Ridge showed up and other dignitaries. Everybody was very respectful, going where they were told, doing what they should have done.

> ' I've seen media behave much worse. '

Mark Stahl of Somerset, Pa., shows a photograph he took of the crash site near Shanksville, Pa., before the area was cordoned off to the media.

Keith Srakocic/The Associated Press

4:37   4:39   4:40

PARK FOREMAN | Technology Security *Consultant*

NEW YORK: I told CNN I could try to download my video over the Internet. It would have taken hours. They had a person in New York who lives about three blocks away. She's a producer for CNN. She scooted down, picked up the tape and then they couldn't use it. She came back for the camera. Not more than an hour or so after they got the camera from me, the video was on the air. About 3 or 3:30 p.m. It was exclusive.

CNN didn't run all the video I shot. Only five seconds of the airplane flying across the city, only the sensational part. They did not show the bodies. They were definitely into the drama and sensational. CNN paid me a lot. It's embarrassing to say, almost a year's salary. I won't tell you (how much). I'm uncomfortable letting people know what my income is.

> ' CNN paid me a lot. It's embarrassing. '

ROBERT A. CUMINS | Documentary Photographer *Black Star*

VERONA, N.J.: I knew I'd better call my agent at Black Star, but she was in Paris. It took 20 minutes to get through to the New York office. They patched me in to the president of Black Star, and we discussed what I had. They got back to me very quickly, indicating that *People* magazine was interested. *People* got the exclusive.

I went home (to Verona, N.J.) to e-mail pictures to Black Star. They said, "*People* wants the picture, but you have to do it in a very large file." I needed to get a CD file five times larger than the one I had so I went back to the lab. A large 18-megabyte file was made for me. I put it in my computer, and a note popped up saying that AOL can't handle anything larger than 16 megabytes. Normally, you get in a car and drive to the city. But you couldn't get out of New York that day; you could not get in.

I call Kinko's, about seven miles away. I'm over at Kinko's working directly on the telephone with my editor at *People*,

Andi Schreiber. I used my cell phone, and to this day I don't know how it held its charge because we were on for an hour and a half. At one point I said to Andi, "You keep saying you want this thing bigger and bigger. Are you talking cover?" The bigger the file, the less grain. I didn't realize they were thinking of using it as a full pullout horizontal two-page cover.

TODD MAISEL | Photographer
(New York) Daily News

NEW YORK: The rest of the day we spent looking for survivors, lugging backboards into the wreckage. Firetrucks were smashed like pancakes. The building remains stood in almost artistic forms that only the devil himself could devise. I was clad in gloves and a helmet from Rescue 2, all of their members missing. Shards of metal ripped my clothes, water was up to my knees from broken water mains. I later ran into Uniformed Fire Officers Association President Peter Gorman and broke down in his arms. I've seen terrible things, but I was overcome with emotions I've never felt before.

> I've seen terrible things, but I was overcome with emotions I've never felt before.

BETH FERTIG | Reporter
WNYC Radio

NEW YORK: I found out where the mayor was. He had gone to a secret location in midtown. I had to walk 30 or 40 blocks north to get there. It was sunny, but you'd look behind you and see smoke in the streets, and everyone on Broadway just standing and looking south. I got a slice of pizza and almost had a nervous breakdown because I had to wait for five minutes to get it. I spent the rest of the afternoon at the mayor's command center. The reporters were trying to figure out what had happened. We were thinking that bombs had brought the buildings down. The mayor talked to us and said he had no evidence of bombs. I just continued to go on the radio all day. I had to call in from a fax machine because the phones at the command center were all in use.

DAN RATHER, NEW YORK: I called my wife and said, "You be the point person for the family. I'm going to be away for a while." I knew that she knew that. We've been together for a long time.

We don't think about food or going to the bathroom. I don't think I had anything to eat until 5 or 6 p.m. I drank "zoom juice," some kind of a protein drink. I don't want to be chewing on the air. At some point, somebody was briefing some official, and Scott Berger, the floor person, said, "If you are going to go to the men's room, this is probably as good a time as any." You just don't think about it.

> This was the first draft of history, and I was a bit player.

AARON BROWN, NEW YORK: I remember David (Bohrman), my producer, saying, "You know, the people who did this are probably watching." I hadn't thought about CNN as the world's news network until then. But he was right — the guys who did this probably are watching. So is the president of France, so is the Russian president. The world is watching. This was the first draft of history, and I was a bit player. Someday my daughter's daughter will hear my description of those events.

TOM FRANKLIN, NEW YORK: There were police roadblocks everywhere. A fire chief came over. He threatened to have John Wheeler and me arrested. We took that into consideration and found another way.

Without much trouble, we were right at Ground Zero. There was mangled metal everywhere, crushed cars, ambulances and firetrucks.

I was prepared to be kicked out of the area at any moment, so I was working real fast, shooting just about anything that I thought was important. It was about 4 p.m., and they were anticipating Seven World Trade Center collapsing. The firemen were leaving en masse. That's where I met James Nachtwey, who was shooting for *Time*. He is a legend in the business, and I introduced myself. We were resting, drinking some water.

I wandered back toward the Ground Zero area. That's

when I noticed these three firemen climbing on top of the wreckage. I realized they were raising a flag. I'm about 100 yards away, and I'm making a long-lens picture. As the flag's going up, I can see a similarity with the Iwo Jima picture that many people have compared it to. I had no idea at the time that it would have any kind of impact, certainly not the impact it had or the comparisons with that famous photograph by (AP photographer) Joe Rosenthal. It happened in an instant.

After they raised the flag, they came down. I didn't bother to get their names because we were really fighting the clock.

'I realized they were raising a flag.'

Thomas E. Franklin/*The Record* (Bergen County, N.J.)

Firefighters raise a U.S. flag amid the smoldering rubble of the World Trade Center disaster.

5:10   5:12   5:17

5:22   5:23   5:24

5:25 P.M. REUTERS NewsAlert: NEW YORK — 47-story 7 WORLD TRADE CENTER collapses.

En Vivo

TELEMUNDO/CHANNEL 47

"EN VIVO"

Liz Gonzalez (with Natalia Cruz): *"That is where the two buildings of the twin towers were. There's a lot of dust here, it's very difficult to be without a mask. That's why you see us with masks, filtering a little bit of the dust that's here. I'd like you to see how much dust is here. This is from the ruins of the World Trade Center."*

LIZ GONZALEZ | General Assignment Reporter
Telemundo/Channel 47

NEW YORK: I found a cameraman, and we talked our way through a police barricade. Visibility was only half a block because of debris and dust. We were next to the fire command station. We started going live, me and (reporter) Natalia (Cruz). They started evacuating the area because they thought a third building was going to go down. We decided to stay. We saw the third building crash. I saw a huge dust cloud coming our way. I screamed, "Let's go, let's go!" and we ran into a public school across the street.

After an hour, they did evacuate the area. It was very intense because we were watching firefighters lying down, exhausted. There were thousands of papers everywhere, and I started rummaging through them. I found people's paychecks from the 82nd floor. I showed them on camera without names. That brought home how awful it was.

Everything was on mine and Natalia's shoulders. They kept coming back to us every 10 minutes for live shots. We must have been live more than 10 times an hour. We were going international. People in Colombia and Peru and Mexico were watching us live.

> ' People in Colombia and Peru and Mexico were watching us live. '

SARA KUGLER | Writer
The Associated Press

NEW YORK: I saw hundreds of firefighters leaning against buildings, sitting on trucks, eating fruit and water that the Red Cross was handing out. "Where are all the injured?" I asked. "They are not letting us in. It's not stable," said the firefighters. They were on the same wavelength as me. They hadn't processed anything. I was talking to Jim Fitzgerald, a reporter from Westchester, who was taking dictation from me. All of a sudden Seven World Trade Center started to collapse. A firefighter started motioning for everyone to run inside. My cell phone cut out. I could hear Jim say, "Sara! Sara! Are you OK? Are you hurt?"

HOWELL RAINES | Executive Editor
The New York Times

NEW YORK: I spent much of the day thinking of things that needed to be done. Sometime between 4 and 5 p.m., I thought that it is all going to come together. The scale was so big. The story was so unimaginably horrible. (Managing editor) Gerald Boyd and I spent a lot of time upstairs looking through hundreds of photos, enough to publish a book. The experience of selecting the best from a body of work like that was moving. I'd seen several pictures of people jumping or falling. Those really got to me. Then there was the image of one man that showed the magnitude of the situation and the loneliness.

One of our editors said, "Are we sure we want to run this? Perhaps it's too close. Close enough that people might be able to tell who it is." It really stopped me. There are certain events so huge that you can't convey them except by one person. It was a correct concern that she had to ask. The picture was about human suffering. In a tragic moment, you cannot be dishonest or evasive. If I had to state it in abstract terms, I thought the picture told a story our readers needed to see. To suppress that picture would be wrong.

> I thought the picture told a story our readers needed to see.

JOHN CARROLL | Editor and Executive Vice President
Los Angeles Times

LOS ANGELES: We trotted out some of our best rewrite people. Each major story went through a rewrite. The major stories were quite sharply done. The craft of rewrite is not so highly valued. I don't know why it's going out of fashion. But having a rewrite person who is not out gathering information, but is sitting in the relative calm of the office and looking at every piece of information coming in, makes for better stories.

FRANK SCANDALE | Editor
The Record, Hackensack, N.J.

HACKENSACK, N.J.: We decided to run the jumper that day as a huge photo on page A5 on the right side. It was three-fourths of the page and at least four columns (wide). We got a lot of heat. We made a decision early on to dominate each page with a large image. That was our general philosophy. To me the jumper showed the utter, complete desperation of the situation that either forced someone to jump or to burn to death. It summed up the absolute terror or despair.

> To me the jumper showed the utter, complete desperation of the situation.

AL ORTIZ | Executive Producer and Director
Special Events, CBS News

NEW YORK: I was in the control room standing for 16 hours. "The Early Show" handled things until 10 a.m. Then me until 6 p.m., then "Evening News" and then "48 Hours." But I stayed involved. I saw my job as keeping a sense of perspective. We needed to keep reminding the audience what we know and what we don't know. We still had no idea whether there were thousands of people dead or tens of thousands. So we were very careful about saying anything about that. I was thinking to myself, "This is the big one. This is about as huge and frightening as it gets."

6:02 P.M. CNN — ANCHOR NIC ROBERTSON REPORTS EXPLOSIONS ROCK KABUL, AFGHANISTAN.

NATALIA CRUZ | Reporter
Telemundo/Channel 47

NEW YORK: What made work difficult was the dust. We couldn't speak because of the dust. When the third building collapsed late in the afternoon, I was live. I was going to keep reporting, but police told me to run. I dropped my mike and said, "I'm sorry, I've got to go," on the air and started to run. My family was watching me on Telemundo Internacional in Colombia. They were very worried.

BETH FERTIG | Reporter
WNYC Radio

NEW YORK: Mark Hilan, the morning announcer, literally kept the station going by himself. He had been at work since 5 a.m. and was live all day. After the building was evacuated, he and two others sneaked back in and negotiated to let us stay. At 5:30 p.m. we lost phone service at the station (near City Hall). They transferred operations to the NPR (National Public Radio) bureau on 42nd Street. We couldn't get a signal out of our building. We have two stations, FM and AM. The FM transmitter was on Tower One, and it was cut immediately (when the tower collapsed). The AM signal operated until 9 or 10 p.m. NPR drove a satellite truck from Washington to help us stay on the air. The chancellor of the Board of Education gave us WNYE-FM as a public service to stay on the air. It was a Herculean feat to stay on the air.

> It was a Herculean feat to stay on the air.

TODD MAISEL | Photographer
(New York) Daily News

NEW YORK: At the end of the day, I sat with several firefighters in the middle of the wreckage, (and we saw) a firefighter's legs sticking out between a crushed firetruck and girders. We wondered who he was, whether he had a family, what company he had come from, and where were his comrades.

JIM PENSIERO | Assistant Managing Editor
The Wall Street Journal

SOUTH BRUNSWICK, N.J.: Our reporters were totally grounded. The New York reporters were having to work virtually. We had retreated 50 miles into the soybean fields, and here we were. People started trickling in, a news editor here, a copy editor here, and we had one graphics person on-site. By about 4 p.m., we had about 30 people, and the stories started coming in. We were all in a mild state of shock, but we're pretty seasoned. We knew we could make a newspaper, and now it was time. Everybody worked at about 150 percent of capacity.

(John) Bussey shows up at about 6:30 p.m. and wants to write a first-person story. I said, "Write it." We didn't get it in the first edition, but it was great, and we put it in the second edition. In the third edition, we moved it up and put it on the front page because it was a hell of a read.

> We moved it up and put it on the front page because it was a hell of a read.

JOHN BUSSEY | Foreign Editor
The Wall Street Journal

SOUTH BRUNSWICK, N.J.: It took me three or four hours to get down there. We were straggling in like refugees coming off a tornado disaster. An editor would come in, and someone would say, "OK, you're the editor for inside, and you're going to be responsible for this."

I started writing. I guess I sat down for two hours or so. I realized that I wanted to get the story in that night because the momentum of the story was the interest that reader would have the very next day, reading what it was like to be close to this event.

PAUL STEIGER | Managing Editor
The Wall Street Journal

NEW YORK: (John) Bussey was the last one out of our building (near the World Trade Center). You know, if I wasn't so gratified he was alive, I would have killed him.

ARIS ECONOMOPOULOS | Staff Photographer
The Star-Ledger,
Newark, N.J.

> One of the ferry guys says to me, 'Go, go! Power to the press!'

NEW YORK: By the end of the day, I lost my note pad. I lost two lenses, over $5,000 worth of gear. While I was walking out, I saw an abandoned fruit stand and took photographs of the fruit covered with grayish dust. I came upon two elderly ladies and a gentleman who had stayed in a building until it was all over, and I took a picture of them walking down the street. I wanted to get their names, so I picked up a piece of paper from the street and wrote their names down. The paper was a confidential memo from American Express.

I walked to Pier 11, where they were ferrying people to Exchange Place (in New Jersey). People on the ferry asked me if I wanted to sit down. I looked bad. My breathing was getting shallow. At Exchange Place, some of the ferry workers told me that anyone who has dust has to go up to Hoboken to get decontaminated. My biggest concern was getting my film back to the paper. One of the ferry guys says to me, "Go, go! Power to the press!" I slipped the cops and walked half a mile to a pay phone to call my desk. I told my editor I needed someone to pick me up.

Office workers Gene Monde, left, and Tina Esposito follow Frank Garone down John Street in Manhattan.

Aris Economopoulos/The Star-Ledger, Newark, N.J.

While I waited, this Jersey City police officer convinced me to go a to a triage station to wash my face. The next thing I knew, they had me in the back of an ambulance headed for St. Francis Hospital. Five people were on me, numbing my eyes, cleaning them, and giving me a painkiller.

(A colleague) picked me up, and I noticed my eyes were sensitive to the light. I looked down at the ground. I couldn't look up because it was too bright. He took me to his apartment, and I took one of the best showers I ever had. We took the PATH train back to Newark Penn Station, which was absolute bedlam with people trying to get out of the city. We ran back to the paper because there were no cabs. Photo editors helped me look over my pictures because my eyes were not good. They almost had to kick me out of the newsroom.

LINGLING SUN | General Manager
China Daily Distribution Corp.

NEW YORK: I got home about 6 p.m. I realized my feet were bleeding. I called Beijing and told them we didn't have an office here anymore. They were worried about me. They asked me if I wanted to write anything and I said, "I can't. I'm too shaken up." They said, "OK, do you mind if we write a story about you?" I thought it was a good idea to let people in China know what was done to us, to this country. They interviewed me over the phone, and the story ran that day on the Internet and on the front page of the paper.

> ' I thought it was a good idea to let people in China know what was done to us, to this country. '

DREX HEIKES | Executive Editor
Los Angeles Times Magazine

LOS ANGELES: By 5 p.m., we'd chartered a Gulfstream with stewardesses and meals. It cost $45,888.81. Two photographers drove across country, and we put their camera equipment and 12 people on the plane. Others drove up from other bureaus. At the height, we had 34 people in the bureau. Normally, there are seven.

YURI KIRILCHENKO | Senior Correspondent, New York Bureau
ITAR-TASS News Agency

NEW YORK: I made four reports, eyewitness reports that the Russian media picked up from our wires.

I think it was dusk when I felt extreme fatigue and a slight, dull pain in my chest. I attributed it to my general tiredness. During my last phone conversation with my bureau chief (Alexi Berezhkoz), I mentioned that I felt terribly dizzy and tired and had some pain in my chest. Fortunately, my wife was in the office and said, "We should go get him immediately." They were stopped by police but managed to get in touch with me on the phone. They gave the phone to one of the police officers and said, "Listen to him." I was moaning and saying something incoherent. It was quite evident that there was a completely sick man on the other end.

Alexi got an armed escort, found me, and brought me to the nearest first-aid station. From then on I don't remember anything. They loaded me into an ambulance and whisked me to St. Vincent's where I was immediately diagnosed with a ruptured aorta. They said I had one hour to live if they didn't start treatment immediately. I was in major surgery for six hours. The doctors said there was a 25 to 30 percent chance of lethal outcome. The doctors said my aorta was genetically weak. Maybe I could have lived with it for my whole life, but under the immense stress, it became a weak spot.

> I was in major surgery for six hours. The doctors said there was a 25 to 30 percent chance of lethal outcome.

SAM BOYLE | New York City Bureau Chief
The Associated Press

NEW YORK: All day you are just making a constant series of assignments, decisions, answering questions. It doesn't lend itself to reflection. People are used to moving quickly, forming into teams, and to immediately sitting down and working side by side. You can be dealing with people inside AP that you don't really know, but you know they understand instinctively the direction and urgency of getting it on the wire.

Scott S. Hamrick | Staff Photographer
The Philadelphia Inquirer

ARLINGTON, Va.: At the Citgo (service station), I had a good view. I took several rolls of film trying to get a helicopter in the foreground with the Pentagon in the background. Now that I had the art, I had to figure out how to get into D.C. to transmit from the office. While I was on the phone a bystander heard that I was from *The Philadelphia Inquirer*, and she introduced herself as an ex-reporter at the *San Jose* (Calif.) *Mercury News*. She asked if she could help in any way. They reopened Interstate 395 into D.C., and after walking one or two miles to her car, she was able to drive into the city and drop me at (the Washington office of Knight Ridder). Knight Ridder didn't have a film processor in service, and no stores were open to process film. Someone said, "Take it to AP." So I had to walk. They kindly processed my film, and I hoofed it back to Knight Ridder for transmission. I was exhausted.

> ' Now that I had the art, I had to figure how to get into D.C. to transmit from the office. '

A helicopter flies near the Pentagon while ambulances and rescue workers wait to tend to victims.

Scott S. Hamrick/The Philadelphia Inquirer

6:36 P.M. **CNN — WHITE HOUSE SAYS PRESIDENT BUSH DID NOT ORDER STRIKE ON AFGHANISTAN.**

TOM FRANKLIN | Photographer
The Record, Hackensack, N.J.

NEW YORK: I had a deadline and knew I had some really powerful stuff. I had an entire day's worth of pictures that I hadn't been able to transmit. I needed to get back to New Jersey. I went back to the marina and had a hard time finding somebody who would take me back to New Jersey. Finally, a Nassau County police boat captain agreed to take me, but he didn't take me where I needed to go. He took me to Liberty State Park, a couple of miles from my car. Once I got off there, I had to go through a decontamination process. I hitched a ride with a woman who really saved me. I explained who I was and begged her for a ride, and she agreed to take me to my car on Route 3.

Once I got back to my car, I started driving back to the office.

The battery on my laptop computer had died. We're all digital, and because I had shot so many pictures earlier in the day, I needed to download. When I went into the city, I left my computer running in my car to download the pictures, and my battery had died. As I was driving back to the office, there was an incredible traffic backup on Route 3.

I drove onto the shoulder, went over some island and pulled into the parking lot of a Radisson hotel. I told them my story. And then I told them that I needed a telephone line and a place to set my computer down where I could plug in because my battery was dead. They gave me everything I needed.

I transmitted my pictures there for the next couple of hours. I had guests in the hotel looking at my pictures. That was an interesting experience because they were giving me good feedback. "Hey, Tom, that's a really good one," and "Oh my God, that's a really bad one!" It was a really unique experience. The flag picture was just one of 40 pictures I transmitted that night. It did not make the front page that day, which I think was a good decision because the readers really needed to see the (immediate) horror of what happened.

> The flag picture was just one of 40 pictures I transmitted that night.

ADAM LISBERG | Staff Writer
The Record, Hackensack, N.J.

NEW YORK: I tried to get to my car. I was pretty sure it was ruined. A cop stopped me. A tugboat had pulled alongside the riverwalk. He said, "It's martial law. Everyone has to get on the boat." I said I was a reporter. He was nice about it. I knew I had to get the film dealt with, and I didn't feel like fighting him.

The boat took me across the river to Jersey City. They were handing out wet towels and bottles of water. The media had a staging center there. Then I took a bus to the train station, but the next train was not going to leave for a half-hour. Fortunately, I had money. I said to a taxi, "I'll pay you $40 to take me to Hackensack." He said, "$80." I said, "OK." I had him drive straight to a photo shop that we use.

I walked back into the newsroom around 5:30 or 6 p.m., wearing the hard hat and the gauze. At that point, I was looking like a terrorist with a bandanna hanging around my neck.

The editor showed me the extra edition and said, "Glad you're back. You've got an hour to write it."

> The editor showed me the extra edition and said, 'Glad you're back. You've got an hour to write it.'

Victims of the World Trade Center disaster and evacuated workers from New York City are unloaded from ferries onto a triage site in New Jersey.

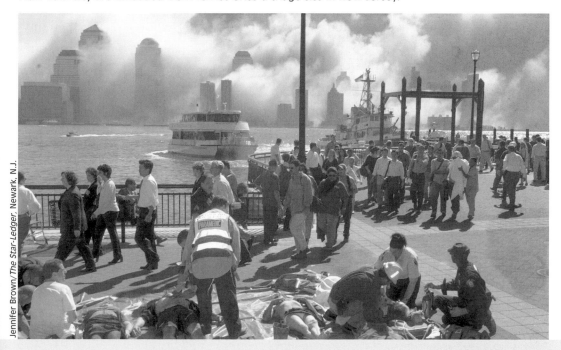

Jennifer Brown/The Star-Ledger, Newark, N.J.

6:44 P.M. **SECRETARY OF DEFENSE DONALD RUMSFELD HOLDS NEWS CONFERENCE AT PENTAGON.**

8:32

8:33 P.M. AP NewsAlert: Washington — Bush says "thousands of lives suddenly ended."

FOX NEWS

Shepard Smith: "*Let's go straight to downtown Manhattan, where the rescue work is now under way. President Bush saying tonight that thousands have lost their lives.*"

MARIANNE McCUNE | Reporter
WNYC Radio

NEW YORK: I managed to get to NYU Medical Center later in the day. Things had slowed there, sadly. A team of triage nurses and doctors were going to another triage center, and I hitched a ride with them on a little four-wheel golf cart. We rode through the city, which was just covered with paper and layers of dust. They went to the other triage center, but there was no one with anything to do.

SHANNON STAPLETON | Photographer
Free-lance

NEW YORK: It got really weird and spooky the later it got. Everyone thought that even Hollywood couldn't make a set like this. At nighttime, you would hear a whistle, dogs would go in, and nobody would come out. I found a tire from the plane. It was about 10 blocks away. I was on such adrenaline. I knew this was the story of a lifetime. That's all I could think about. I didn't even get tired because I knew I was documenting history.

> I knew this was the story of a lifetime. That's all I could think about.

MARTY GLEMBOTZKY | **Photographer**
WABC-TV

> All my things that made me who I am as a photographer, were lost.

NEW YORK: It was not until that night, when we sneaked back to get video to freshen up the piece for the 11 p.m. (newscast), that I thought to find my truck. We shot night video of the burning hulk, which is all it was. I went over to the area where I thought I had parked my truck. As I got closer, I saw guys in flak jackets with big guns come up. And they were saying, "No, no, no."

The truck became a metaphor for my experience. They never found my truck. I believe it was crushed in the collapse of Seven World Trade that afternoon. All my possessions, my briefcase, my rain gear, all my things that made me who I am as a photographer, were lost. In a way, I never really felt a sense of completeness because I never found my truck. In comparison to the loss of thousands of lives, my truck is insignificant. The station paid me for possessions. The truck had 130,000 miles on it. It was old.

Hours after the attack, an American flag flies near the site of the World Trade Center disaster.

Doug Kanter/Agence France-Presse

TOM BROKAW | Anchor and Managing Editor
NBC News

NEW YORK: Adrenaline is a very, very powerful drug. My friends said, "My God, you didn't even go to the bathroom." I get into a zone. It's hard to describe. You are out there sitting at the end of this powerful, but fragile, electronic gangplank. One false step and you plunge into the deep, dark sea. The only conscious thought I had was this old astronaut mantra: "Don't screw this up!" I'm not thinking. It's all instinct. I'm grateful I was at this age (61) and stage of my career. I had a certain perspective having been through a lot in my career, and I needed every fiber of all I'd been through that day.

> ❝ You are out there sitting at the end of this powerful, but fragile, electronic gangplank. ❞

GERALDINE BAUM | Reporter
Los Angeles Times

NEW YORK: I said to a cop in a car, "What's the most direct way to get to Park Avenue South?" He asked, "You want a ride?" I got in the back of the cruiser. He blurted out, "We lost the day tour. We lost our whole day tour," and he started to cry. He took me right to the office. I work a block from the Empire State Building. I asked, "What shall I do tomorrow?" Dean Baquet, managing editor in L.A., was on a speakerphone. Dean said, "Focus in, Geraldine. Do one precinct." That was a really good idea.

JIM PENSIERO | Assistant Managing Editor
The Wall Street Journal

SOUTH BRUNSWICK, N.J.: We pushed the first deadline back to 8:30 p.m. Then we came back at 9:45 p.m. and did a second edition. At about 11:40 p.m., we did a final. It was a great effort. I assembled the staff, and I thanked them all. Under the circumstances, I thought it was an extraordinary paper. Just because we were rocked on our heels didn't stop us from being *Journal* people. I think it's a good news organization when you stress it to see what it's made out of.

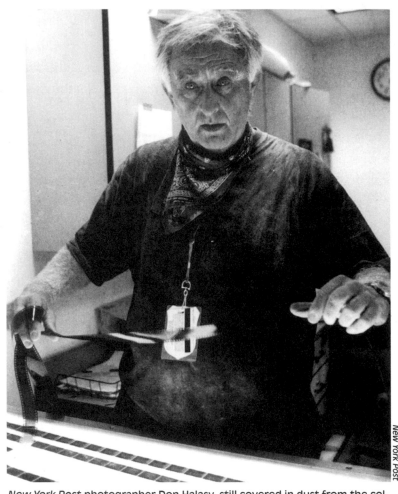

New York Post

New York Post photographer Don Halasy, still covered in dust from the collapse of the second tower, checks the film he took of the disaster.

DON HALASY | Photographer
New York Post

> They had a psychiatrist so I stopped in to talk. I talked for about two hours.

NEW YORK: The memory that stays with me is nobody being around when I dug myself out. There had been two dozen people out there, and when I got out, there was nobody standing but me. I started yelling, "Does anybody need help?" and there was dead silence. It was like being in hell. It was black, I could not see anything, and I kept calling out. (He cries.) Later, I got an assignment at Bellevue Hospital where families were looking for bodies. I'm walking around and I'm starting to cry. They had a psychiatrist so I stopped in to talk. I talked for about two hours. They let you vent.

JESSE LEWIS | National Copy Chief
The Wall Street Journal

SOUTH BRUNSWICK, N.J.: When you think about the fact that your base is gone and people are scattered and no one really knows what's going on, just getting the paper out that day is remarkable. It was really a hard thing to do, and it was really hard to get through it emotionally, because every now and then you'd just have to stop. Everybody came through, and everybody came through while being in shock.

CATHERINE FITZPATRICK | Fashion Writer
Milwaukee Journal Sentinel

NEW YORK: The fashion shows are in Bryant Park, tucked behind the New York Public Library. They erect these enormous white tents that accommodate lighting and sound systems with fountains gurgling water. I went by the tents that night. The gates to that end of the park were closed and locked. There was one security guard on duty. A notice typed on paper said something like, "Because of the events, the rest of the week is canceled." I made notes on the litter that was blowing about. The goody bags put on the chairs were still there. It struck me how incredibly frivolous that world is. And how very different the day went.

ROD DREHER | Columnist
New York Post

NEW YORK: I went out to water the plants in the back yard. There was an airplane ticket from the World Trade Center sitting in our garden. It was from May. My wife, Julie, and I went to a Lebanese Catholic church memorial that night. Some of the people there had grown up in Beirut, and they told us, "Once you smell burning human flesh, you never forget that smell. That was the smell over Brooklyn today." I realized then what was in the ash that was covering our back yard.

> Once you smell burning human flesh, you never forget that smell. That was the smell over Brooklyn today.

9:22 P.M. CNN — PENTAGON FIRE CONSIDERED CONTAINED BUT NOT UNDER CONTROL.

KILEY ARMSTRONG | Assignment Editor, New York Bureau
The Associated Press

NEW YORK: My 7-year-old daughter's school called me. I told them, "Do me a favor, call my husband and tell him I won't be home tonight." I didn't know until two days later that my daughter's school had been evacuated because it was next to a reservoir that serves New York City.

ADAM LISBERG | Staff Writer
The Record, Hackensack, N.J.

> ❛ I was thinking that this is the biggest news I've ever witnessed in my life and I have to write the best story of my life. ❜

HACKENSACK, N.J.: I sat down at the computer, and I was just stunned. We have writing rooms where you can go to avoid the chatter of the newsroom. It was so hard to focus. At the time, I was thinking that this is the biggest news I've ever witnessed in my life, and I have to write the best story of my life. I'm a damn good writer when I'm at my best, but I was shellshocked. I wrote it because you always end up managing to write. My friends said they could hear my voice in it, but I'm still not happy with it. Most of me said, "Adam, you ran for your life, you saw things that no one should ever have to see. It's OK that you didn't write the most compelling piece of literature."

Then I was stuck in New Jersey and couldn't get home to New York. I borrowed a reporter's car and went to Sears around 8:45 p.m. and bought some cheap sneakers, sweats to sleep in, a pair of jeans and a clean shirt. The paper rented rooms for anyone stranded. I threw away everything I was wearing that day. I kept the hard hat and the canvas L.L. Bean bag I was carrying. At midnight in this hotel room, I finally stepped into the shower. I could see the dirt running down the drain. I got out, and I could see my ears were filled with dust.

The next morning, I pop awake at 6 a.m. I go to the office. They start making plans for me to do rewrite. I say, "I can't do this. I have to go home. I can't focus. I can't think. I can't write." They said, "OK, go home."

SARA KUGLER | Writer
The Associated Press

NEW YORK: They opened the auditorium (of a nearby high school) for cops and firefighters to rest. I decided that would be a good place to hang out. When the first reports of missing firemen came in, I was going into the auditorium. I didn't know about any missing or dead firefighters. I went up to a group of them and said, "I'm a reporter. Can I just talk to you?"

The first three said they didn't want to talk. The fourth guy yelled at me, "Get out of my face! Leave me alone!" Another guy in charge kicked me out of the auditorium. He followed me out, screaming that I can't come back in. I felt it wasn't necessary to scream at me. I didn't once try to protest. He kept saying, "Keep going. Farther. Farther."

> ❛ I'm a reporter. Can I just talk to you? ❜

PAUL DISNEY | Photographer
Soldiers

ARLINGTON, Va.: The Military District of Washington Engineer Company had been activated to search for survivors. I'd worked with this unit for about a year and a half. I'd gotten really tight with some of these guys. As soon as I found out they were activated, I went back down to the Pentagon.

I got inside the perimeter they had set up and walked over to where my buddies had their headquarters tent. We started talking. They hadn't been able to hear any news. They'd gotten there about 11:30 a.m. and didn't even know the towers had fallen. I managed to get a rescue suit from one of my buddies and went to the Red Cross tent to get blankets for all of us. We slept a little away from the helicopter pad. There were all sorts of bright lights, and you heard all the commotion and tools they were using. One of my buddies, Sergeant Fredericko Ruiz, couldn't sleep. I got a shot of him, propped up on one arm looking back at the hole.

MOLLY BINGHAM | Photographer
Free-lance

ARLINGTON, Va.: I was in Virginia at a training course for journalists and AID (Agency for International Development) workers in conflict situations. *The New Yorker* called me around noon or 2 p.m. and asked me to shoot at the Pentagon. I was concerned I couldn't get into town because of roads being closed. I was about two hours away. So I waited until around 7 p.m., went home and got my gear. I ended up at the Pentagon around 11:30 p.m. (A nearby) Citgo station had become this ad hoc media center. There were about 30 or 40 people there. I used to be (former Vice President Al) Gore's official photographer, and some of the most entertaining photos from that whole period are of the press doing what they do: filing stories, inventing an office, inventing a set someplace where news is suddenly happening. I have pictures of a Fox (TV) guy, who was reporting from the top of an eight-foot ladder. I like shooting behind-the-scenes stuff of how the press makes what we see on TV.

MOLLY RILEY | News Assistant
Reuters

> I've got this gaping, smoking hole ... how can I capture this best?

ARLINGTON, Va.: I went back to the Pentagon with a real camera and long lens and shot pictures that had flames pouring out of the spotlight on the damaged area. That picture was used a lot. I never looked at the scene as, "Oh my God, I can't believe this!" It was more like, "OK, I've got this gaping, smoking hole with flames coming out of windows. How can I capture this best?" It's a different mind-set.

WTTG Fox 5 reporter Bob Barnard sits atop an eight-foot ladder he found in a dumpster at a gas station near the Pentagon. From the ladder, he could give "live" reports with an unobstructed view of the Pentagon behind him.

Molly Bingham

9:57 P.M. CNN — NYC MAYOR GIULIANI SAYS CITY SCHOOLS WILL BE CLOSED WEDNESDAY.

10:27 P.M. **AP** NEWSALERT: NEW YORK — MAYOR SAYS SOME PEOPLE ALIVE IN TRADE CENTER.

AMERICA **UNDER ATTACK**
NYPD: THERE ARE PEOPLE ALIVE IN
THE BUILDINGS

...GES AMERICANS TO RALLY BEHIND PRESIDENT BUSH

CNN LIVE — BREAKING NEWS

AMERICA UNDER ATTACK

Paula Zahn: *"An untold number of victims are still trapped inside the wreckage of the building. Mayor Giuliani and the police chief confirming they believe there are people who are still alive."*

PETER JENNINGS | Anchor and Senior Editor
ABC News

NEW YORK: This is another of those events which we shall always remember where we were at that moment we learned what was happening. This sounds self-serving, but I've been through a very large number of crises with ABC in (what seems like) 146 years or so that I've been here, and I have one overwhelming impression from this experience. In an age when journalism is contracting, you lose at your peril those who are really expert at their jobs.

Our investigative unit is not on the air every day. In the current television environment, some people think they should be a vulnerable component in tight times. But on that day, John Miller, Brian Ross, Pierre Thomas — our extremely valuable Justice Department correspondent — and Chris Isham, who runs the unit, were just extraordinary. If you don't have them on your team when this hits, you really suffer. While people tend to say the anchor was on for 17 hours and did a good or bad job, what the anchorperson did is important, but what I did is a byproduct of the news division.

God forbid you should be inexperienced on a day like this.

> God forbid you should be inexperienced on a day like this.

GERALD M. BOYD | Managing Editor
The New York Times

' What's really hard for people to understand is what it means to put out a newspaper in the middle of this. '

NEW YORK: What I've learned from this experience is what a tremendous, tremendous institution *The New York Times* is. From the business side that rallies to support us, though it means throwing out ads; to the publisher who doesn't bat an eye about committing the resources; to reporters and editors who automatically go to the scene. And editors who are turned back by the Coast Guard trying to get over here and then work at home, and people who kept working even when they could not reach their families and didn't know what was going on. In some cases, people suffered losses. They had relatives who were missing and are missing. Yet they kept working. They kept working that first day, then the second day, then the third day. It's truly extraordinary.

I think what's really hard for people to understand is what it means to put out a newspaper in the middle of this. I know journalists in New York truly experienced that.

People stand in line September 12 to buy *The New York Times* from a news truck outside the newspaper's Times Square offices.

Victoria S. Vila/*The New York Times*

10:39   10:41   10:45

ARIS ECONOMOPOULOS | Staff Photographer
The Star-Ledger,
Newark, N.J.

NEW YORK: I partially lost the first layer of the cornea in my left eye. I knew my eyes were in trouble, so I went to the ophthalmologist. I had microscopic shards of glass embedded in my eyelids. (He later recovered from the injuries.)

I went to a friend's wedding. It was really important for me to see happiness. I felt numb. I got depressed and sad for a while, but then I was fine. I have a little note to myself, folded in my wallet. It says, "Thank God you're alive. Appreciate every day of your life and realize how lucky you are to be blessed by ones who love you."

> ' I partially lost the first layer of the cornea in my left eye. '

BOLÍVAR ARELLANO | Photographer
New York Post

NEW YORK: I survived massacres and covered civil wars in Ecuador and Colombia and (El) Salvador. I've seen everything a human can do to another human being. I thought I had seen everything until this happened. I was crying day and night remembering those lives lost for no reason. It was the first time my kids saw me crying.

NANCY GABRINER | Editorial Producer
ABC News

NEW YORK: We went off the air about 2:30 a.m. I just assumed I would go out, get a cab and go home. That just shows how insulated I was from the whole thing. I walked to Central Park West and stood in the street. There was not a car or a person. I felt like I was in a science fiction movie. I thought something would come along, but nothing came. That was the moment I realized I had no sense of what was happening outside the building. I knew it was happening, but not right outside, not to the people I knew. There's definitely a distance that comes with this job. In some respect, you almost feel cheated out of experiencing certain events.

0:49 P.M. CNN — ATTY. GEN. ASHCROFT SAYS THERE WERE 3 TO 5 HIJACKERS WITH KNIVES ON EACH PLANE.

ELINOR TATUM | Publisher and Editor in Chief
New York Amsterdam News

NEW YORK: We kept our run the same, about 35,000 papers. There were no deliveries below 14th Street. On Thursday afternoon, I delivered our newspaper in the general vicinity of where I live in the East Village to about 20 newsstands. A friend helped push the cart. I borrowed it from my mother. We probably hand-delivered 150 papers. Six hours later, everyone I brought papers to had sold out. That never happens.

SUSAN WATTS | Photographer
(New York) Daily News

> I'd go to sleep and wake up and see bodies jumping out of windows.

NEW YORK: I came home and drank so much wine it was like drinking water. It didn't even take the edge off. I couldn't sleep. I'd go to sleep and wake up and see bodies jumping out of windows.

I had a situation three years ago on an assignment for *Life* magazine where the reporter and I got kidnapped and robbed in Central America. These gunmen were going to shoot us, but somehow we escaped and ran into the woods, where we hid for about 15 hours while the gunmen hunted for us. When I came back from Honduras, everyone said, "You had your near-death experience." Like, "It's smooth sailing from now on, Susan!" But after the moments of terror I experienced on September 11, Honduras was a walk in the park.

HOWELL RAINES | Executive Editor
The New York Times

NEW YORK: Between 5 and 9 p.m., it was inspirational. You could see this paper being created before your eyes. It was like watching a birth. This event is so horrible that it is difficult to talk about the moment as fulfilling. But I had the feeling as a journalist that I was in the exact right place. I've been a journalist for 37 years. Everything up to this point had prepared me for this moment.

MARIANNE McCUNE | Reporter
WNYC Radio

NEW YORK: They wanted me to do the overnight (shift). My husband brought me Rollerblades (in-line skates), and I skated all over the city. I went to the morgue where they were registering names of those who were missing. That was just horrible. I have a memory of a woman standing in front of one of the hospitals with a list of people who had been hospitalized in New York City. The list was very short. There was a woman standing in front of her, crying and begging her to read it over and over again.

CAROL MARIN | Contributor
CBS News

NEW YORK: I got in the shower and my feet stung. I realized I had lost skin off some of my toes. Professionally, it was people doing what they were supposed to do. If firefighters could be in there losing colleagues, it seems like the least everyone else could do was follow suit. I'm still looking for the one who saved me.

I remember seeing this giant ball of fire come out of the earth as I heard this roar and thinking, "Who's going to explain to my kids that I needed to be at the World Trade Center on this day?"

> ❛ Who's going to explain to my kids that I needed to be at the World Trade Center on this day? ❜

SARA KUGLER | Writer
The Associated Press

NEW YORK: When we came into the school, all the rescue workers, volunteers and media threw their bags in a pile. Someone stole my cell phone and wallet. I called and canceled my debit card while others were calling their families. I had no money.

I think I was asleep by 3 a.m. Wednesday. I'd been up about 32 hours. I never got my cell phone back, but somebody found my wallet with my license and mailed it to me.

ARTHUR SANTANA | D.C. Superior Court Reporter
The Washington Post

ARLINGTON, Va.: I was looking for the opportunity to tell the story through somebody else. I ended up finding Ken Foster that night and talking to him. (Foster sneaked inside the perimeter to look for his wife, who worked at the Pentagon.)

About daybreak, I went up to Ken Foster again and asked if I could tell his amazing story of searching for his wife (who was killed in the attack). We found a Metrobus that the Red Cross commandeered. We were disheveled, hungry and tired. I can't begin to compare my plight to his. He was heartbroken, devastated. I was in awe of this man, of what he was doing.

I found myself again struggling between being a reporter and a person. As I'm writing and taking notes, I'm torn at times, having to put my notebook down and talk to this guy man to man, trying to understand what he was saying without writing it down. There are moments like that when you have to stop being a reporter and be a human being. You can write it down later.

> There are moments when you have to stop being a reporter and be a human being.

PAUL DISNEY | Photographer
Soldiers

ARLINGTON, Va.: The next morning, around 8 a.m., I went in with a team to do a secondary search for bodies. They gave me a device that if you stop moving for 30 seconds, it will let out an alarm. We started walking into the Pentagon, single file. If you didn't have a flashlight, it was pitch-black.

We started seeing giant orange X's that someone had spray painted. At the top of the X, you'd see the unit that had been there and the number of dead people they'd discovered. The largest amount I saw was 19 DOAs (dead on arrival) confirmed. If you'd gone in earlier, you'd have seen 19 dead bodies. I was taking photos the whole time except when I was searching for bodies.

At one point, we actually got into where the aircraft had ceased all forward movement. The biggest part of the aircraft I saw was two feet by eight feet. I didn't bother to look inside to see if there were any bodies. Apparently, there were.

I managed to hook up with a first sergeant. He pulled me into a room. There were three Army officers who had died of smoke inhalation, I'm assuming, because they weren't burned.

I've seen six bodies in four years of being a photojournalist, three at the Pentagon. It sounds like a cliché, but September 11 really changed my life. I got to the point where I want to give something back to society. It sounds corny, but I want to try to get into volunteer firefighting. Before, I was just ditty-bopping along, trying to make photos that somebody would pay me to keep taking.

> ❝ I've seen six bodies in four years of being a photojournalist, three at the Pentagon. ❞

A rescue worker inside the Pentagon crash site marks an area where bodies were found.

Paul Disney/*Soldiers*

PAUL STEIGER | Managing Editor
The Wall Street Journal

NEW YORK: This was the violence of war wreaked on an unsuspecting civilian population, right in front of my eyes. So it had a huge visceral impact. Of course, it's going to change the way we think about our lives, change our economy, change our politics. Everything was in those few moments transformed.

I'm just enormously proud of what we accomplished. It was a fantastic accomplishment, not just for the journalists but for the technology and production people. We got all kinds of calls and messages of congratulations from people in the industry but also from ordinary readers. They said it was such a comfort to have *The Wall Street Journal* published at all. The fact that the paper was so complete and so good made them feel that their lives were still connected. That makes you feel that you're useful.

> The fact that the paper was ... so good made them feel that their lives were still connected.

TOM BROKAW | Anchor and Managing Editor
NBC News

NEW YORK: I got home at 2 a.m., sat down and was staring out the window. I had a big stiff drink of scotch. I was trying to process lots of feelings. What we'd been through. Where it goes from here. How as an American and a New Yorker it was affecting me. How did we do today? My God, there was amazing work done today. I've got to remember to say something to so-and-so who did an amazing job.

I was curiously contained and controlled when I got home. I was doing this out-of-body examination and asking myself, "Why am I not melting down?" So I had a second drink, and it went straight through me. I went to sleep. I slept for four hours and woke up, and the alcohol had no effect on me. I felt rested. Then a phone call came. A very close friend of mine died of congestive heart failure the night before. It just released something in me. For half an hour, all the emotion that I'd bottled up came out. I just sobbed.

JOHN DEL GIORNO | Helicopter Reporter
Metro Networks/Shadow Broadcasting, WABC-TV

NEW YORK: I think that live TV withstood its biggest test. The vast majority of reporters did an amazing job under absolutely incredible conditions. As a journalist, you're really a historian, because people 200 and 300 years from now are going to look back at how we recorded it. In the back of your mind you knew that the city was going to be a different place. You had an emptiness inside of you because you knew that the city was permanently changed.

> Live TV withstood its biggest test.

JOANNE LIPMAN | Weekend Journal Editor
The Wall Street Journal

NEW YORK: The next morning was my daughter's 11th birthday. I was buying a present for her in the Trade Center when it happened. It was refrigerator magnets for my daughter's locker, the last little thing I was looking for. I have a receipt from Lechter's in the Trade Center from 8:55 a.m. The plane hit at 8:46 a.m. Buying presents for her probably saved my life. Liberty Street, where I would have been walking to my office, got all this burning debris dumped on it.

The next morning I gave her that morning's paper, sat down and explained how it came out. I explained how proud I was of all the people I work with, how proud I was of the paper, and how brave all the people I work with are. I will carry that forever.

ROBERT A. CUMINS | Documentary Photographer
Black Star

VERONA, N.J.: That moment was completely by chance for me. One thing I think about very often is why was it me that made this picture (of the second plane striking the building)? I've been photographing professionally for 34 years. I'm very involved in photography of the Middle East and Israel. It's just very confusing why it was me that made that photograph.

SHANNON STAPLETON | Photographer
Free-lance

NEW YORK: I got a letter faxed to the Reuters office from the family of Father (Mychal) Judge thanking me for such a compassionate photo (see page 99). They said it gave them a sense of closure and made an impact on their lives that he was at such peace. The sister of one of the policemen who were carrying Father Judge also called to thank me. I got choked up. I thought I was going to get this "you uncompassionate son of a bitch" stuff. It helped me a lot.

MAGGIE FARLEY | Bureau Chief, U.N./Canada
Los Angeles Times

NEW YORK: That night, trying to go to sleep, I could not turn my brain off, replaying the scenes I saw during the day. Like a lot of people, there are just going to be moments when you are working along, working on adrenaline, and you see something or hear something, and your eyes fill with tears.

The baby (Farley was eight months pregnant on September 11) was very active. It felt like she was moving all the time. I was wearing police tags. She kept kicking, and the tags would jump up. It was very reassuring actually. I felt this strong presence of life amid the presence of death and devastation. When people asked how I feel bringing a child into a world like this, all I could say is life continues. I think we are going to name her Zoe, which means "life" in Greek. (Zoe Brauchli was born on October 28, 2001.)

TODD MAISEL | Photographer
(New York) Daily News

NEW YORK: It was a day that will change my perspective on life and the business forever, with every familiar face heaven-sent and every photo shoot becoming a sacred obligation — a documentation of history so important as to be practically religious in nature.

> It was a day that will change my perspective on life and the business forever.

ADAM LISBERG | Staff Writer
The Record, Hackensack, N.J.

NEW YORK: That next night, after I interviewed some people and called in some notes, I got over to TriBeCa. All the streetlights are out. I see cars parked along the street that are clearly damaged. I recognize my car by the license plate. They'd towed the other cars. I felt like that scene in Jimmy Stewart's (movie) "It's a Wonderful Life." My car! My car's here!

The windshield is intact, but cracked. All the other windows are blown out. Six inches to a foot of dust, debris and paper are in the car. The sides are dented and pitted. The rear lights are cracked. It's not drivable. As I'm digging this stuff out, these two *Daily News* reporters wander by and one says, "Dude, your car!" I said, "Man, this car is nothing. I don't care about the car. I'm glad to be alive."

BETH FERTIG | Reporter
WNYC Radio

NEW YORK: I went home at 5 a.m. Because I lived in the "frozen zone," the police wouldn't let me take a taxi past 14th Street. I had to walk about a mile home. The streets were completely deserted. I'm walking home, the towers aren't there, and I am just sobbing hysterically. I get to Washington Square Park, and there was a homeless man sitting outside on a bench.

He asked me, "Why are you crying?" I said, "Look behind you" (to where the towers once stood). He goes, "It's not the end of the world." That just made me cry more.

I called my mother, slept three hours, got up and went back to work.

> I'm walking home, the towers aren't there, and I am just sobbing hysterically.

HERNANDO REYES SMIEKER | Reporter
Noticias 1380

NEW YORK: I didn't work for two days because I didn't feel so good. I cried like a baby again and couldn't go on the air.

MARTY GLEMBOTZKY | Photographer
WABC-TV

> ❛ It was a brutal story to report. ❜

NEW YORK: I had to go to St. Vincent's and hang out with the people who were waiting for their loved ones with pictures. You know that their loved ones are dead, but they are acting like they are going to come back. It is really hard to put a good piece together when you are penned in with people who are standing there waiting for ambulances to come bringing their loved ones who are not coming. I was trying to portray the images properly, yet I was suffering emotionally. It was a brutal story to report.

I did start to shut down after a few days. I shot less and less. People would beg me to put their loved one on television, and I would not roll. I would just pretend I was shooting.

I have recovered. I feel better. I do my job. I prefer to do feature stuff. I do not want to do Ground Zero anymore.

Below, Rachel Uchitel searches for fiancé, James Andrew O'Grady, outside Bellevue Hospital in Manhattan; right, top: Adolfo Rodriguez holds a photo of his missing father, Alexis Leduc; right, bottom: Claudia Trevor comforts Liz Gallello, holding flyers with a picture of their missing friend, Amy O'Doherty.

Andrew Vaughan/The Associated Press/CP

Wally Santana/The Associated Press

Edward A. Ornelas/The Associated Press

HAROLD DOW | Correspondent
"48 Hours," CBS News

NEW YORK: I literally ran for my life two times that day. I've been in the business a long time, and I have never covered anything like this in my life. I don't think anyone has. I've been to Beirut when it was a war zone, the Soviet Union, covered hurricanes where thousands of people were being evacuated and my crew and I were the only ones headed into the storm.

It was sheer terror running for my life, but I never really had time to understand the magnitude of it all. It finally hit me when I was off the following Friday and everything replayed in my mind. I went to church and thanked the Lord.

The media were very much a part of the terrorists' plan. From the time the first plane went in, they gave the media time to get down there to record the second plane. These pictures were shown all over the world, that's their trophy. That's the sad part.

> ❛ The media were very much a part of the terrorists' plan. ❜

JIM PENSIERO | Assistant Managing Editor
The Wall Street Journal

SOUTH BRUNSWICK, N.J.: The adrenaline jag you get from working makes you keep going. When we stopped working, I felt like I had a hangover. Not from drinking, but from this sort of very deep sadness. Anger and sadness.

AL ORTIZ | Executive Producer and Director
Special Events, CBS News

NEW YORK: I really did try to put my own feelings second. I was in there to do a job. In the little tiny gaps, and believe me they were tiny, I felt angry, upset and scared. I knew people weren't coming home that night.

I live in New Jersey and had gotten in at 8:15 a.m. or else I wouldn't have been able to get to work at all. As bad as it was, that would have been worse.

DAVID HANDSCHUH | Photographer *(New York) Daily News*

> It's not natural to witness this stuff through the viewfinder of your camera.

NEW YORK: Photographers who survived physically — how do they do psychologically? It's not natural to witness this stuff through the viewfinder of your camera. You witness it a second time, while you're editing it. Then you're re-exposed to the trauma when you view your picture in the paper the next day, or if you have a picture that's really become an icon for an event like this, when it's used over and over again on the second anniversary, the fifth anniversary, the 10th anniversary. Photographers need to talk to other photographers about stuff like this and make sure that we are all OK mentally.

GERALDINE BAUM | Reporter *Los Angeles Times*

NEW YORK: Finally I called (my husband) Mike (Oreskes, a *New York Times* editor), but he couldn't leave. He had the car. I was damned if I was going to walk home. Mike said, "Why don't you come over and get the car?" It was 10 p.m. It was positively spooky outside. I was kind of scared. No one was on the streets. I met a couple in their 30s. They both worked in the investment business, and I said, "Would you walk with me?" The kindness of others was really important to me. I saw Mike. He gave me a hug. We didn't really say a lot. We were both stunned. I looked at Mike, who is my best friend, and thought, "Oh my God, he was scared too."

I got home. The nanny was there. My daughter looked at me, "Mommy, your hair is gray!" My hair was covered in soot. I was so freaked out. I took a hot, hot shower. I put on a pair of white pajamas. I woke my son up. "I'm scared, Mommy," he said. When I saw the raw terror in his eyes, I realized I was the parent, and I couldn't reassure him. I took both kids and put them in bed with me.

I've covered a lot of big stories, and it's a lot of fun. We often get a detached, professional satisfaction out of people suffering. There was not one moment this was fun or enjoyable. Though there were lots of reporters here from L.A. and lots of camaraderie, I'd do anything to go back to September 10. I'm a reporter through and through, but there's not one bone in my body that doesn't wish this never happened.

KRISTEN BROCHMANN | Photographer
Free-lance

NEW YORK: It's taken me a long time to reconcile how I feel about this photograph. This is not the kind of photograph I'm known for, and it's now my most famous photograph. And it might be the most famous photograph I have ever taken. My name might be indelibly linked with September 11, and yet I didn't lose anybody. The only way I could sort of reconcile my good fortune is that I was able to take a record of this for everybody else to see. Lots of other horrible things happen (such as) ethnic cleansing, and there's no record. This is what it looked like, and this is what it was. I'm very ambivalent. People who see the photo will say, "Wow, it's a really great photograph." But it's a really horrible thing that happened, but I'm happy I was able to capture it.

> ❛ This is what it looked like, and this is what it was. ❜

The New York Times' Howell Raines and Steve Berman examine a slide and digital image of Kristen Brochmann's photo.

Barbara Alper

DAVE WINSLOW | Correspondent
The Associated Press

ARLINGTON, Va.: I drove around to get a perspective. There were police everywhere. Smoke was still billowing over the Pentagon. Then I hear this very deep sound of air-raid sirens, which I hadn't heard for 30 years. I can tell you honestly that when I went to work the next day and talked to my boss, I was still suffering from a form of post-traumatic stress. I still had tightness in my stomach, this sense of nervousness, depression. Getting back to work the next day after that first 36 hours relieved it.

TOM FRANKLIN | Photographer
The Record, Hackensack, N.J.

HACKENSACK, N.J.: It was an extremely emotional day for me. I never cried on an assignment before, and I cried half a dozen times that day, not so much about what I saw, but for what this meant and how our lives would never be the same.

I've received hundreds of e-mails a day about the flag photograph. It made me immediately aware of how powerful the picture is and that it might actually be something that helps people. We've also received thousands of phone calls from people wanting to get the picture. The company set up a way in which people can get the picture and, hopefully, make a donation. We're very hopeful that we'll be able to raise a lot of money with this photograph. I think it makes people feel a little stronger about being American.

> I never cried on an assignment before, and I cried half a dozen times that day.

YURI KIRILCHENKO | Senior Correspondent, New York Bureau
ITAR-TASS News Agency

NEW YORK: After I regained consciousness, pictures of what I had seen haunted me for quite a while. When you are lying alone in a hospital ward, you remember the most dramatic events. The most dramatic event of my life was the experience of being so close to that collapsing tower.

GULNARA SAMOILOVA | Photo Retouch Artist
The Associated Press

NEW YORK: I'm from Bashkortostan, a Muslim republic in Russia. I'm a Muslim myself, born Muslim, not practicing. I came here nine years ago. Love brought me here, but we separated. I was very upset that the towers were gone. I've lived all these years downtown. I used to see them from my bedroom window. I felt personally that I lost something that day.

RICHARD DREW | Photographer
The Associated Press

NEW YORK: I relive it every day.

MARTIN WOLK | Business Reporter
MSNBC.com

NEW YORK: I felt very much disconnected. We're the number one news Web site, but we have a very small news staff. I felt very much on my own. I felt part-victim, part-reporter. The next morning one of the editors reached me at my brother's on the Upper West Side and asked if I would go back down and cover Ground Zero. I'd been up since 4:30 a.m. crying and trying to come to grips with everything that had happened. I said, "No." I'd made a decision to go home to Seattle. I decided I'd rent a car and drive to Cleveland, where my parents live, and keep going. I just wanted to get out of Manhattan. You didn't know what was going to happen next. I didn't think I could risk staying and getting sucked into the vortex of this story.

> I felt part-victim, part-reporter.

WENDY DOREMUS | Widow of
Photojournalist William Biggart

NEW YORK: He didn't come home. I was hysterical. I kept trying to call him on the cell (phone) and kept getting his voice mail. It was pandemonium.

It's like all of life changed that day.

Index of Names and Organizations

Page numbers in italics refer to photographs.